MOUNTAIN BIKING

MOUNTAIN BIKING

THE ULTIMATE GUIDE
TO THE ULTIMATE RIDE

Bill Strickland

R·M·P

Mc Graw Hill

CAMDEN, MAINE • NEW YORK • SAN FRANCISCO • WASHINGTON, D.C. • AUCKLAND
BOGOTÁ • CARACAS • LISBON • LONDON • MADRID • MEXICO CITY • MILAN • MONTRÉAL
NEW DELHI • SAN JUAN • SINGAPORE • SYDNEY • TOKYO • TORONTO

Ragged Mountain Press

A Division of The McGraw-Hill Companies

10 9 8 7 6 5 4 3 2 1

Library of Congress Cataloging-in-Publication Data
Strickland, Bill, 1964-
      Mountain biking : the ultimate guide to the ultimate ride / Bill Strickland.
          p.   cm.
   Includes index.
   ISBN 0-07-038703-6
   1. All terrain cycling.   I. Title
GV1056.S79 1998
796.6'3—dc21   98-3014
                                      CIP

Questions regarding the content of this book should be addressed to:
Ragged Mountain Press
P.O. Box 220
Camden, ME 04843
www.raggedmountainpress.com

Questions regarding the ordering of this book should be addressed to:
The McGraw-Hill Companies
Customer Service Department
P.O. Box 547
Blacklick, OH 43004
Retail customers: 1-800-262-4729
Bookstores: 1-800-722-4726
www.books.mcgraw-hill.com

Printed by Quebecor Printing, Fairfield, PA
Edited by Kathryn Mallien; Gerald Novesky
Design by Design Associates, Chicago, IL
Production by Publisher's Design and Production Services, Inc., Sagamore Beach, MA
All Illustrations by John Hinderliter, Pittsburgh, PA
Chapter Opener photos by Bill Strickand, all other photos as credited.

This book is intended to educate and encourage beginning and intermediate recreational
mountain bikers. The author has attempted to make it as informative and accurate as possible; however, there may be errors of omission. Mountain biking is dangerous, especially at
high speeds or wherever there is the possibility of collision with hikers, animals, trees,
inanimate objects, or other cyclists. Always wear protective gear and obey all recommended
safety rules. Before starting a cycling training regimen, be sure to consult your physician.
The author and publisher take no responsibility and are not liable for any person who is in-
jured while mountain biking.

CONTENTS

FOREWORD BY SUSAN DEMATTEI VII

ACKNOWLEDGMENTS VIII

1 WELCOME TO MOUNTAIN BIKING 1

2 GEAR WITHOUT FEAR: HOW TO BUY COOL BIKES AND EQUIPMENT 7

Let the Biker Beware 8

Attention, Off-Road Shoppers! 9

Gear and Clothing without Fear and Loathing 16

Pedal Principles 21

To Repair Is Human 22

3 BECOMING AN EARTHSURFER: BASIC MOUNTAIN BIKING SKILLS 25

The First Fifteen Minutes 26

Loose Rules 27

Position of Power 28

Finding a Line 29

Braking News 31

Get Over It 34

Get a Grip 37

Going Up 39

The Decent Descent 44

Turn, Baby, Turn 46

Life in the Balance 48

Fuel for Thought 50

Shred Lightly 53

Go Your Own Way 54

BILL STRICKLAND

4 SHRED U: HIGHER STUDIES IN GETTING HONED   55

An . . . ticipation   56

Not Missing Links   57

Rise and Shine   57

Radical Descents   61

Lunge Time   63

Air Apparent   64

One Good Turn   66

Narrow Minded   71

Unbraking   72

Funky Terrain   74

Speed Thrills   81

Spin Cycle   83

Crash Course   84

5 RIDING ON THE EDGE: EXPERT SKILLS AND BEYOND   87

Personal Style   88

Jumping for Joy   90

How to Not Jump   91

Maximum Braking   93

When Feet Are Faster   94

6 THE BALLISTIC BALLET: TRAINING AND RACING   97

Your First Race   98

Anatomy of a Plan   101

7 RIDING FOR ADVENTURE   108

The Small and the Classic   109

Getting Your Bike There   115

8 OUT THERE: WHY MOUNTAIN BIKING MATTERS   119

APPENDIX: RESOURCES   123

INDEX   127

SKIP BROWN, OUTSIDE IMAGES

FOREWORD

I fell in love with mountain biking in 1986, shortly after plunking down what seemed then to be an extravagant $450 for a new bike. It was a beautiful, sparkly sky blue. Never mind that I didn't know anything about the brakes, the components, the feel of the saddle. I just wanted a colorful new mountain bike.

Some friends of mine in the bike-crazy town of Chico, California, had been raving about these new "off-road" bicycles. What the heck—I figured I'd give it a try. Of course, my bike didn't touch dirt for the first three months I owned it, and when I finally ventured onto singletrack I wanted only to climb; the bumpy, rocky descents petrified me, and I avoided them whenever possible.

But I did have a knack for climbing, and I was reasonably fit from lots of road riding, so I did pretty well. Or as well as my bad technique would allow. I learned slowly, by endless and sometimes painful trial and error. And I started racing.

My lack of descending skills was my usual undoing in those early races. But there weren't any comprehensive books about mountain biking, and I couldn't figure out what I was doing wrong. I'd lose and simply assume I was a poor descender by nature. Trial and error. Trial and error. Another lost race, another spill.

I did eventually figure it out, and it took only a few years. Some good riders and lots of persistence helped. I began racing professionally, got a spot on the 1996 Olympic team, and even earned a bronze medal. But I still wonder what a book like this one would have done for me during those years of learning.

I'm still looking for ways to improve my technique, to understand how I'm riding. I emulate riders who display the kind of smooth, efficient control of their bikes that Bill advocates in this book. And I ride a lot. Face it: Learning the skills of mountain biking takes practice, no matter how experienced a rider you are. But understanding the "hows and whys" of the skills will enable you to uncover your talent sooner—and with fewer bruises—leaving you more time to concentrate on the sights and sounds around you. The anecdotes and experiences you'll find in this book, coupled with hard-earned learning and sound advice, will help you reach the places you want to go—literally!

Over the years I've seen the sport of mountain biking change thousands of people's lives, including my own. You gain confidence and self-esteem by challenging your body and your mind during the course of a ride; you become more adventurous by exploring the world around you in search of beautiful terrain; you meet wonderful people; you improve your health; you use your bike as clean, economical transportation; and—most importantly—you have fun.

Read this book, practice what you've read, and enjoy those rides. It makes me grin just thinking about it!

—Susan DeMattei
1996 Olympic medalist

ACKNOWLEDGMENTS

Eternal dirt to Dondo and Tim, who rode with me when I was stupid and slow;

to *Mountain Bike* magazine, the greatest off-road publication ever, which paid me

to learn how to ride and how to explain how to ride (most of my skills lessons

were originally inflicted on *Mountain Bike* readers); to Beth, who will ride with

me forever; and to my sister Leann, for reminding me that we should never stop

trying to improve.

WELCOME TO MOUNTAIN BIKING

On Sunday morning the fat guy who's been drinking beer after every lap is kneeling beside his bike, one arm thrown over the top tube, praying. Fast, soft, desperate, his supplication comes to me: *Never again, never again, never again . . .*

I don't know if his words are a request or a promise, don't know if they're about the beer or the biking (or the combination), or even if they're directed to his god, his body, or the sensible voice inside that tries to stop us from doing things like mountain biking. If his brain is as addled as mine, he probably doesn't know any of those things, either.

It's 10:39 in the morning on a June day hot enough to explode an inflated bike tire left too long baking in the West Virginia sun. I'm about to experience the single best ride of my mountain biking life—the ride where everything comes together and I become the easy honed bike dude of my dreams—and at the same time become a loser. On the greatest ride of my life I'm about to disgrace my four teammates by disqualifying us from the 24 Hours of Canaan Mountain Bike Race.

But I don't know that yet. I'm standing in the staging area, waiting for one of my teammates to finish his lap and give me our baton. Canaan—which, appropriately, rhymes with insane—is a team relay run from noon Saturday to noon Sunday. You ride a lap, check in at the staging area, where an official marks your time and hands the baton to your team's next rider, then you stuff some fuel down your throat and try to sleep for an hour before your next lap.

The race course, which winds up and down West Virginia's northern Mononga-hela National Forest, is a killer. On foot, you sprint from the staging area to the bike pit. Within 50 pedal strokes you plow into an ascent steep enough to push even the pro riders off their bikes. The single-track is a highlight film of harsh Eastern-style trails—rocks, roots, whoop-dees,

Anyone can become a mountain biker, but the process is quicker—and more fun—if you have help.

BILL STRICKLAND

Get ready to ride fast, stay
loose, and fall a little in
love with the unexpected.

grass that sucks all speed from your wheels, fallen logs, water, mud, ooze, slime, muck, grit, grime, and plain old dirt.

There's also a two-mile climb on a rutted logging road to the course's high point. From the peak you plunge into a thousand-foot drop of slick sidehills, mossy boulder fields, trails that thread through trees barely a handlebar-width apart, and off-camber, high-speed turns that conspire with your momentum to flick you off the side of the mountain.

It is pure, total, uncensored hell. Which means it's knobby heaven. Especially when the sun goes to bed before you do. Riding at night, on an eight-inch-wide trail illuminated only by a wavery light mounted on your handlebar, you might be the last person on earth. Nightmare images spring into your cocoon of dreamy light: A log

black as death, a puddle shaped like the lake you almost drowned in when you were six years old. You question your bike handling, your fitness, your sanity, and why you are carbo-loading with cold spaghetti at 3:14 A.M.

Then, finally, an hour and 21 minutes before the whole thing is over, you find yourself waiting at the bottom of a mountain to ride your team's last lap, your body and brain so shot you begin to chant the only words that seem to make sense: *Never again, never again, never again . . .*

As I mumble those words I see a familiar red-and-yellow jersey pop out of the woods high above and I bend down to tighten my shoes against my swollen feet so I can pedal. This is it. Last lap. My first go-round was the team's fastest—1:17—but as we fatigued our lap times ticked down to 1:30, 1:40, at night some of us

A Brief History of Grime

People have always ridden bikes on dirt—the first bicycles were invented in the era of unpaved roads. Those highwheelers had only one gear, no way to freewheel (coast by letting the wheel spin without also spinning the pedals), and saddles that perched riders six feet or higher in the air. Even so, cyclists rode highwheelers on dirt roads, through forests, across deserts, over mountain paths—pretty much everywhere we do today.

What you and I think of as mountain biking began sometime between 1971 and 1974 in Marin County, California. A dozen or so road racers craved relief from their regimented training and hard-core lifestyle. They began pulling 1940s Schwinn Excelsior cruisers—curvy, fat-tubed, balloon-tired "paperboy" bikes—from trash heaps and cobwebbed garages. After restoring the bikes to working condition, the riders threw them into the beds of pickup trucks and drove to the top of Mt. Tamalpais, where they staged impromptu races down dirt trails and roads.

The most popular route was nicknamed Repack because the friction generated during the 2.1-mile drop would sizzle the grease out of the bikes' coaster-brake hubs, requiring a teardown and grease repack after every run. Calling themselves "klunkers," "ballooners," and "fat-tire flyers" (the phrase "mountain bike" wouldn't be coined until 1979), the mainstream dropouts bombed down Repack in jeans and flannel shirts, wearing thick work gloves and boots and no helmets. At the bottom they drank beer, smoked dope, and awarded hand-sewn ribbons and trophies made from broken bike parts. They were the only mountain bikers in the world.

"We were just having fun," says Joe Breeze, one of those original racers (and the one who later built the first true mountain bike frame—lighter, but sturdier and stronger than the Excelsior frames that kept breaking underneath the riders). "People think there was some marketing genius behind the development of mountain bikes, but we were just having fun."

In 1977, Breeze built the first full rig made exclusively for mountain biking: a 38-pound, rigid-fork, 18-speed "Breezer" that sold for $750. (Today a $750 bike comes with a suspension fork and 24-speed gearing and weighs somewhere between 25 and 28 pounds.) Breeze sold ten of those first mountain bikes. Everyone who saw one wanted one. Today more than eight million mountain bikes are sold every year in the United States alone.

Almost all of those Marin maniacs are still around—some, like Breeze, Gary Fisher, and Tom Ritchey, are still pushing the technology with their own bikes and components.

Racing is still central to the sport, but now it's done on a world-class level in the Olympics, in a series of continent-hopping World Cup events that crown an overall champion, and in a one-day world championship race that earns the winner a hallowed rainbow jersey to wear for one year. Besides down-

continued on page 5

even close to 2:00. There's no way I'll finish before the noon cut-off, which means no one will have to ride again. So everyone else is showering and putting on non-riding clothes. Returning to earth.

On the bike, I have nothing. My legs are weights I cannot lift. My lungs are heavy, filled with something that prevents them from taking in any air. Blisters at the base of all my fingers squish against the rubber grips of my handlebar.

But something is happening. As fatigue strips away some senses, others appear—ones I've absorbed but never used. As I come off the first climb I can suddenly see the good lines of the trail as if they're marked with fluorescent paint. I carve a switchback I'd walked on every previous lap, and a spectator whistles and says to his friend, "That's how you ride it."

What the hell? I'm blasting across a field of crushing rollers, then shifting into the middle ring when I hit the logging road. I'm passing some riders, then every rider I see.

How am I doing this? Who locked my tray table in the upright position and decided it was time to take off? It wasn't me. I'm not the pilot on this flight.

As I crest the final ascent, I see Beth, my wife (and teammate), who rode the chairlift up to snap some photos. She seems surprised. "Fourteen minutes," she shouts at me. She means, "Don't finish any sooner, you idiot." But my fatigue makes the words mean, "You can do it. Go faster and you'll be my hero."

I do go faster somehow, surfing everything the trail throws under my wheels, riding every inch of the downhill I couldn't clean when I was fresh and rested. Beneath my wheels, trail rages like a prizefight. Above, where I live like I never have before, life is smooth, easy, fun. I sling out of the final turn like some kind of freaky metal cat.

My teammate Mike stands there. "Don't cross the line," he yells. "Don't cross the line!" I hear, "You have a great line! You have a great line!" And then I blaze into the staging area, log in at 11:58, and disqualify my team because, technically, we quit racing before noon.

I lost. I blew the entire team's effort. I wasted 23 hours and 58 minutes of dedication (and sleep deprivation). But it was fantastic.

For an hour and 19 minutes I became the mountain biker I'd spent my life trying to become—the smooth-flowing mountain biker we all imagine ourselves to be. Winning or losing weren't as important as simply riding, feeling the trail spin beneath me like it belonged there and had always been there and always would be there. I finally got out of my own way and became a real mountain biker. If I had to lose a million races to strip off that protective coating again, I'd do it.

You will, too, once you know the feeling of riding like a true mountain biker.

Mountain biking combines the cool, edgy mystique of surfing with the regular-people accessibility of bowling. Offroad riding will be one of the wildest, most thrilling adrenaline rushes you'll ever experience—yet it can be enjoyed safely by just about anyone, just about anywhere. (You don't even need a mountain—honest.)

When you become a mountain biker you will be able to ride trails you could not walk safely. You will have the fitness and handling skill to pedal yourself atop mountains two miles above sea level. You will ride deep into woods, down canyons, across red plateaus that don't end at this horizon, through meadows of wildflowers as high as your shoulder. You will hit speeds so fast that afterward the truth will sound bogus even to you (ah, but you were there). You will know the still, silent moment at the top of an airborne arc when all life waits for your next move.

You will also learn more about your neighborhood than you ever thought possible, because one of the greatest things

continued from page 4

hilling, there's cross-country, dual-slalom, trials (obstacle riding), 24-hour races, triple-digit–mileage endurance events, stage races like the Tour de France VTT, races across Alaskan ice, the Australia Outback, mountains in Nepal, jungles of Borneo, and every place else you can imagine.

And, just as when that first fat tire hit Repack, the sport is still about escape—perhaps even more so in our contemporary world of instant everything and constant information assault. Mountain biking is about one person out somewhere riding, or sharing singletrack with just a few friends who know how to be alone together. There's another kind of escape, too—release and abandon, freedom to roam, permission to play.

Added to escape is tribalism. Mountain bikes are totems that unite outdoor adventurers, counterculture treadheads, hard-core athletes, throttle-twisting immigrants from motocross, body-piercers and other societal extremists in search of the fringe, environmentalists, and a lot of real people with real jobs who can shred the edge only on weekends—a more diverse group than you'd find, say, on a golf course. That's one of the coolest things about mountain biking.

There are also more places to ride today—partly because suspension, better brakes, and lighter bikes make it possible for more people to ride terrain once reserved only for the elite, partly because, despite trail closures that began in 1983 and continue today, there are more places to ride simply because there are more riders creating them. The International Mountain Bicycling Association opens more than 700 miles of trails to mountain bikes every year. Ski resorts have discovered the glory of summer income: About 150 of the more than 400 ski areas in the country have mountain biking programs—for a fee riders get access to groomed trails, free lifts to the top, maps, and sometimes riding lessons.

There has never been a better time to be a mountain biker.

about mountain biking is that it's like the coyote: It thrives everywhere, even in urban jungles, even where responsible people have done their best to eradicate it. You will find secret trails in city parks, hidden routes in the scrub behind buildings, half-hour rides just minutes from your home that you can sneak off to when you need to escape life for a while and get tired and muddy.

You will know all of these things and more when you become a mountain biker—when you stop being just another person on a bike with fat, knobby tires.

It's true that anyone can become a mountain biker, but the process is much quicker—and much more fun—if you have help. Offroad riding is a skill-intensive sport that requires lots of techniques and tricks. Most of these radical moves are simple to understand and to learn if someone shows you how, but difficult to accomplish untutored.

That's what this book is for. I'll introduce you to the sport—the basic skills (and a few advanced ones), the equipment, the great rides, the funky history. I'll take you on your first ride and hang right there with you to explain why you got hung up on that log or how those confusing shifter things work. I'll know just when to push the pace or when to stop atop a mountain to take a breather and soak up the killer view. (I might even save you from a wreck or two. No promises, though.)

There are three skills chapters in this book—beginner, intermediate, and ad-

vanced. The first two cover many of the same techniques, but in the intermediate section you'll learn how to refine the things you were introduced to earlier—how to ride faster, farther, smoother, and safer. The advanced chapter deals with gonzo techniques and introduces some "riding philosophies." Don't get turned off by that last phrase. It's actually kind of a cool concept. At its highest skill levels, mountain biking becomes about style, and major improvements are more likely to come from changing how you think about the trail than from learning a new riding technique.

If that sounds a little funky, well, that's mountain biking. Get ready for it. Get ready to ride fast, stay loose, fall a little in love with the unexpected, and lie beneath an open sky with your chest heaving. You're about to become a mountain biker.

GEAR WITHOUT FEAR: HOW TO BUY COOL BIKES AND EQUIPMENT

YOU are the important component. You're the motor—and the pilot. Without power and guidance even the fanciest bike is nothing. It goes nowhere.

A pro on a rusty Huffy will grind an amateur on a $5,000 full-suspension marvel. If you remember this undeniable and too-often unvoiced truth—*the rider matters more than the bike*—you won't become one of those boneheads who take credit for all the good rides but blame equipment for all the bad ones.

Even so, your gear is anything but irrelevant. Equipment is as integral a part of mountain biking as the trails—or riders. For one thing, between the extremes of a pro on a beater and an overtricked first-timer, equipment has a significant effect on performance. With the right stuff (not necessarily the most expensive) you will ride faster, longer, and safer. And you will ride more because your gear inspires you to.

Equipment is cool, which is something old-school retrogrouch riders try to make mountain bikers feel bad about. Don't listen to them. Your gear is something beyond simple possession. You will bond with your bike, buy things for it, feel bad when you neglect it. You will mourn your favorite pair of ripped shorts, hang onto your first gloves long after they've become unusable, ascribe mystical powers to a certain set of tires. That's part of mountain biking, in its own way as wonderful a part as grooving a trail or nailing a turn or spiking a jump.

Let the Biker Beware

The beauty—and problem—with mountain bike technology is that it evolves so fast. Last year's breakthrough is this year's yawn and next year's joke. So instead of recommending models and brands that go out of date as soon as the catalogues are mailed, this chapter gives you the inside knowledge you need to decide what this year's best stuff and best bargains are—no matter what year it is.

One thing you won't find here are recommendations for specific components. When you're trying to decide between twist shifters and push shifters and other freaky incarnations, or between sidepull cantilever brakes and disc brakes, the ex-

THE MOUNTAIN BIKE

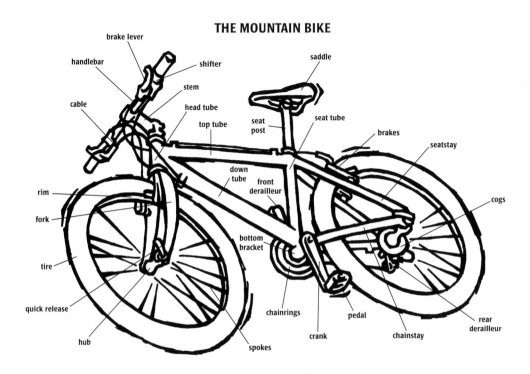

perts at your local bike shop are the best resource. They'll be able to match the intricacies of the latest technology with your personal style and budget.

This chapter will help you decide whether you should ride front- or full-suspension, what kind of fork suits your riding style, if you should buy traditional pedals or clipless, which accessories are necessities and which are chi-chi. You'll even be able to work your way around your bike with a wrench without doing too much damage (and perhaps even fixing a problem or two).

Attention, Off-Road Shoppers!

There are three kinds of mountain bikes—rigid (also called unsuspended), hardtails, and full-suspension (also called softtails or dual-suspension).

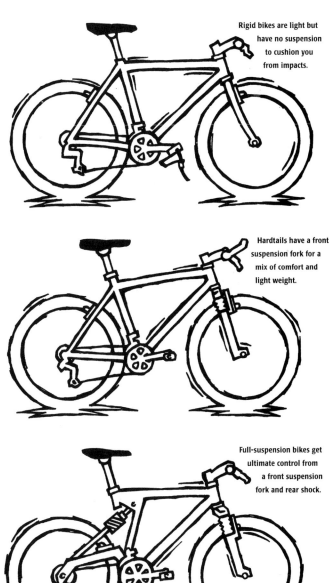

Rigid bikes are light but have no suspension to cushion you from impacts.

Hardtails have a front suspension fork for a mix of comfort and light weight.

* **Rigid bikes** have traditional, triangle-shaped frames; they don't use any kind of frame-mounted suspension to cushion the rider from impacts. Purists love getting the true feel of the earth, but a rigid bike mean less control and more fatigue because of the undampened pounding. Except for some special applications (such as trials riding, a highly technical form of competition), rigid bikes are most suited for riders who won't venture beyond smooth bike paths or easy trails.

* A **hardtail** uses a front suspension fork to absorb shock, giving the rider more control and less fatigue without a significant weight penalty (a suspension fork weighs about one to two pounds more than a traditional, rigid fork) or increase in cost. Hardtails excel at cross-country racing and all-around rides where climbing and cruising fast are as important as descending.

* **Full-suspension** bikes have a suspension fork in front and a shock absorber in the rear, a combination that suspends the rider completely for maximum com-

Full-suspension bikes get ultimate control from a front suspension fork and rear shock.

The high-pivot URT sucks up big hits but feels rough on small chatters.

A low-pivot URT is a good descender but a poor climber.

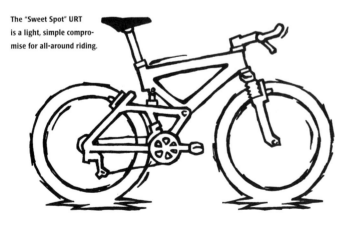

The "Sweet Spot" URT is a light, simple compromise for all-around riding.

fort and control. That's the good part. But in general, full-suspension bikes weigh more, require more maintenance, and cost more than hardtails or rigid bikes. Some designs "bob" during pedaling or waste a rider's energy in other ways. Most designs are made specifically for bombing downhill, although more are made for cross-country riding every year. If you're interested in a full-suspension bike, be sure to get one made for the type of riding you'll do most—either downhilling or all-around cross-country hammering.

Suspension Style

Bikes are fitted with rear suspension in all kinds of configurations and freaky designs. They all work, but some will be better suited to your riding style than others. Here's a guide to the most popular rear-suspension designs.

* **High-Pivot Unified Rear Triangle**. A unified rear triangle (URT) means that the bottom bracket—thus the cranks and chainrings—are part of the suspension device, so the entire drivetrain moves with the suspension. This eliminates erratic motion or bouncing that can occur if the rear of the bike moves but the pedals don't. URTs are also simple designs—one pivot.

  There's more. A high-pivot URT sucks up big, rolling hits (though it feels harsh when you land after jumping), but it doesn't modulate well on lots of small bumps—it feels chattery. But because pedaling drives the suspended rear wheel into the ground, it's the best climbing design I've ever ridden. Good for cross-country riders, bad for downhillers.

* **Low-Pivot Unified Rear Triangle**. Instead of driving the rear wheel to hug the ground like you do when you pedal a high-pivot URT, this design wants to *lift* the rear. This hurts climbing performance and adds just a bit of bobbing,

but it makes for freaky fun descending. Buy and fly.

* **Sweet-Spot Unified Rear Triangle**. This URT has one pivot between the high and low positions. That means a sweet spot rides like a plush downhill bike when you're seated, then "locks out" and climbs or sprints like a hard-tail when you get out of the saddle. It's a light, simple, sweet compromise for cross-country riders.

* **Linkage**. These are complex designs that look like Erector sets. All those links and tubes mean your rear wheel can absorb many different kinds of shocks by traveling through lots of curves instead of a simple arc as with other suspension designs. Although they're heavier than other designs, more prone to wear and breakdown, and require lots of maintenance, linkages have lots of travel, little wasted energy, or other problems. They make excellent all-around bikes—good for downhillers as well as cross-country riders who don't mind a few extra pounds.

* **McPherson Strut**. This simple design has a pivot at the rear axle and no other complicated linkages. The design is light, simple, wastes almost none of your energy, absorbs big and small hits—but never feels truly plush. It's a performance feel—like cornering in a BMW instead of in the family sedan. An outstanding cross-country design.

* **Swingarm**. This is a simple idea—a single swingarm that arcs upward to absorb shock—with many mutations. Depending on where the swingarm pivot attaches to the bike, pedaling affects the motion more than in any other design. Most bike makers put the pivot at about the height of the middle chainring, which neutralizes unwanted action most often and still leaves the bike plush, but ride character is all over the place. Be sure to put plenty of test-

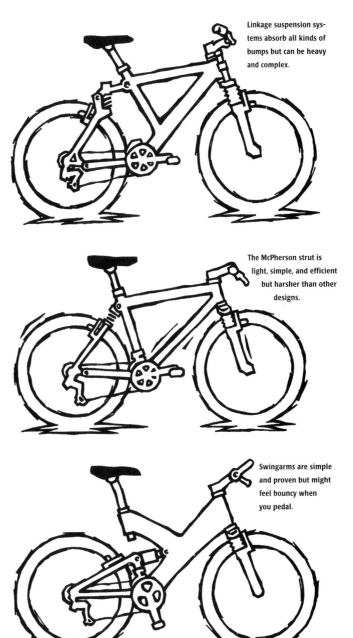

Linkage suspension systems absorb all kinds of bumps but can be heavy and complex.

The McPherson strut is light, simple, and efficient but harsher than other designs.

Swingarms are simple and proven but might feel bouncy when you pedal.

DH OR XC?

A full-suspension bike designed primarily for downhilling has features that will make you miserable on a cross-country ride (where you'll be doing a lot of climbing and cruising along terrain that requires extensive pedaling). Downhill bikes are shorter and smaller—for better control when descending at high speeds—but force you into a riding position that will make you feel cramped on long rides. They're also heavier, lack the low gears for climbing steep hills, have huge, aggressive tire treads that only slow you down on a cross-country ride, and might not have a place to mount water bottles. They sure look cool, though. Just don't get seduced by moto style if you'll regret it on your first ride.

With a shorter cockpit, downhill bikes put you in an upright position for more control on killer descents—but are too heavy for cross-country riding.

ride time on any swingarm bike you're interested in to make sure it matches your style.

How Much Bike for Your Buck?

If the world were as perfect as mountain biking is, the quality of your rig would be determined by your desire instead of your dollars.

Life, unfortunately, is cash and carry. Facing that cruel reality, a caveat: When you want a new car you don't go to Wal-Mart (not yet, anyway). So when you want a bike, don't go to a department store. First, the quality is crappy, even if you're coughing up $200 or more: You're not getting a real mountain bike with a solid frame and precise shifting and braking. Second, the personnel probably know nothing about fitting you to the right size bike. Third, the assembly is sloppy. And finally, there's no friendly expert you can return to for minor tune-ups and advice—routine service supplied by all bike shops. You won't have to spend more at a bike shop, but you'll get more.

Here's a guide to what kind of bike you'll get at common price points.

* **Under $300.** Frames are predominantly straight-gauge chromoly steel, with some "high-tensile" steel—the cheap stuff. If you've ridden anything better, a $250 bike feels like a tank; if you're coming off a Huffy, the thing will be a dream. The riding position is compact and upright—like the entire bike, more suited to cruising paved bike paths and parks than shredding mountains. Components are low-level, mass-market quality—reliable shifting and braking under casual conditions, but nothing you'd want to stress with a season of racing or hard-core hammering. The chainrings, cogs, and other parts are more prone to wear than higher-level gear would be. Headsets, handlebar, stem, and other parts are likely to be no-namers. You might not even get toe clips and straps, let alone clipless pedals. Forget suspension (it's out there but you don't want it at this price). Go rigid.

* **$300–$500.** This is the bottom level of what could be considered a "real" mountain bike. You should be able to find an aluminum or butted steel frame (butting makes a tube lighter and stronger by shaving material from un-stressed areas) designed to give you a more aggressive riding position and better control. Tires have big treads for traction; pedals have clips (or they might be low-level clipless); goodies like saddles and grips will carry cool name brands. Components are a mix

THE MOUNTAIN BIKER

of mid- and low-level stuff. That's okay, but maximize the mid-level quality: Get a bike with its best components in the drivetrain (shifters, derailleurs, and cranks). Don't settle for a bottom-line suspension fork in this range; you should be getting something mid-level, with adjustability. Full-suspension isn't a good buy at this price.

✺ **$500–$700.** These are race-quality bikes, true thrashers that will take whatever abuse you and the mountain throw in front of their tires. Most frames in this category are oversized, butted aluminum for more strength

TAKE THE RIGHT FORK

Besides light weight and lateral stiffness, what you want from a suspension fork is the ability to control the speed of compression and rebound: You want to be able to *dial in* a fork so it moves fast enough to absorb lots of little chattering bumps but still has the plushness to suck up a big hit. Don't worry too much about the fork's innards—bike makers change the technology at hyperspeed. There are air/oil, coil-spring, open-bath oil, coil-and-air, electronically controlled forks, and incomprehensible marvels that just months after their release seem to become as boring as toasters. Whatever the technology, make sure you get the most adjustable fork your budget can hack. That's the real secret.

and lightness. There are fewer steel frames here—an inequity due more to economics than quality (it's costlier to produce a steel frame that's as light as aluminum). Components are mid-level picks that give crisp shifting and braking—not as crisp as the top-end stuff (and not as durable), but 90 percent as good at 50 percent (or less) of the price. Starting here you'll also find quality wheels with 32 spokes (lighter and stronger) and brand names on the seat post, bar ends, saddle, and stem. Rigid bikes at this price rock—excellent frames and components—but nobody buys them anymore because suspension has become so good (forks used to suck unless you paid at least $750). Full-suspension bikes are tempting, but they really don't kick into quality mode until $750 or higher. Dig deeper if you want full bounce.

* **$700–$1,200.** This price range contains the best buys in mountain biking.

MATERIAL WORLD

Although the design of a bike—the lengths of the tubes and the angles at which they're joined—affects ride quality more than what it's made from, there are some generalizations that may help you decide what frame material would be best for your style and budget.

* **Steel** is the benchmark, offering a good balance of rigidity, comfort, strength, and weight. And because it's been around so long, bike makers know how to get the most out of it for the least cost. The one downer: rust.
* **Aluminum** is harsher than steel (at least in today's oversized tubes) and batters some riders away, although this is less of an issue with suspension. It gives the same strength as steel for less weight. It never rusts, either.
* **Titanium** has a phenomenal strength-to-weight ratio and gives a resilient ride. "Aluminum weight, steel ride" is the idea, except the feel is even livelier. It also has the highest resistance to impact dents. No rust, either.
* **Composites** such as carbon fiber, metal matrix, and thermoplastics have the highest stiffness-to-weight ratio, which makes them light but harsh—perfect for suspension setups. Composites also dampen vibration, a ride sensation some cyclists like and others call dead. Try it and see.

Beyond this you pay more and more money for smaller and smaller advantages. You should be able to get a bike to fill any purpose—whether you're a cross-country racer, a downhill fiend, an all-day epic hound who demands comfort, or a city guerrilla who needs something with a little flash. Besides aluminum, look for composites and the least-expensive titanium frames. There might even be some thermoplastic floating around. Components will be one notch below the best. Don't settle for anything but clipless pedals.

* **$1,200–$1,500.** Bikes in this range are for committed riders who forget about the rest of their lives come April (whether it's due to racing or this season's life-threatening epic), equipment freaks, lightness geeks who measure a bike's worthiness by grams, and dabblers with lots of cash. Nothing wrong with any of those groups, except they have better bikes than most of us do. Frames of all materials have cool features—curved chainstays, gussets, and other tricks to increase strength and drop weight. Full-suspension bikes at this price have the same tasty specs that hardtails had at $700–$1,200. There are also nice touches—embroidered seats, work-of-art head tube badges, and top-line clipless pedals.
* **$1,500 and up.** When you're ready to spend this much, you won't need to consult this chapter anymore—or if this is your first bike and you have that kind of jack you can hire me as a personal advisor.

Having a Fit

The thing that most affects how well you and your mountain bike will ride together is not suspension, frame material, shifters, brakes or other components, or even cost.

The ultimate relationship is *fit*. If your bike fits you, you will ride safer, faster, more often (because you won't ache as much), and look cooler. Bad fit screams poser.

When you buy a bike at a bike shop, it'll be fit to you just like a tailor fits your clothes. There might be some alterations: changing the stem length, tweaking the saddle up, down, backward, forward, maybe chopping the handlebar. This will help you understand what's going on.

* **Standover height**. When you're standing on a level surface, straddling the top tube in your riding shoes, there should be two to four inches of clearance between your crotch and the frame.

(Think for a second and you'll understand why that's important.)

* **Saddle height**. The seat should be raised or lowered until your knees are slightly bent at the bottom of the pedal stroke. (Here's a great guideline for adjusting the saddle height after you've ridden a while: If the front of your knee hurts, the saddle's too low; if the back hurts, it's too high.)

* **Saddle tilt**. A level saddle is a wondrous thing, neither squashing your crotch nor sliding you forward toward the handlebar. Some riders go with a slight upward tilt to help them sit back and lessen the strain on their arms.

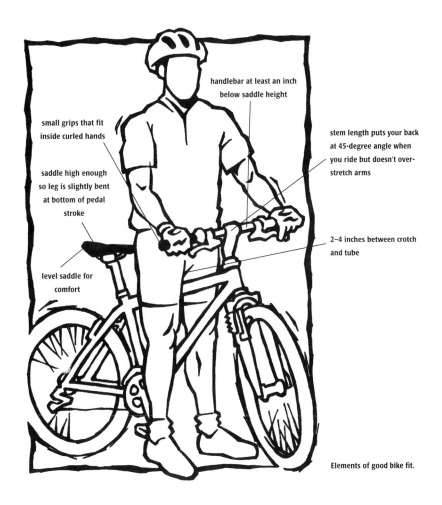

handlebar at least an inch below saddle height

small grips that fit inside curled hands

stem length puts your back at 45-degree angle when you ride but doesn't over-stretch arms

saddle high enough so leg is slightly bent at bottom of pedal stroke

level saddle for comfort

2–4 inches between crotch and tube

Elements of good bike fit.

Some riders, most often women, slightly tilt their saddles downward to relieve the presure of the saddle's nose against the crotch. Start level. (If no position is comfortable and you've also tried a wider saddle as described in the "saddle width" section that follows, you might try a saddle with a hole cut in the nose to relieve pressure.)

* **Saddle width.** Narrow racing saddles look fast and cool, but if the slim profile doesn't match the width of your "sit bones," you'll be putting all your weight on soft tissues. If you experience numbness in the crotch, consider a wider saddle. Don't mistake normal ache for numbness, however. If you're a new rider, your crotch will need two to four weeks before it stops aching after rides.

* **Saddle position fore and aft**. The saddle should be slid along its rails until your knee is directly over the pedal axle when your foot is at the 3 o'clock position and you're sitting normally. (There's a special setup to measure this at bike shops.) Some riders adjust the saddle slightly rearward for better leverage when pushing big gears. Again, start with the standard.

* **Stem height**. Honed cross-country riders set their stems at least an inch or two below the top of the saddle. This helps put weight on the front wheel for climbing and gives adequate control. Downhill riders set their stems higher. Novices sometimes begin with their stems even with the top of the saddle and then move it down as they become used to riding and can stretch out more.

* **Stem length**. This helps you adjust the cockpit length—the distance from the saddle to the handlebar. For cross-country riding your back should be bent about 45 degrees (for the best pedaling efficiency combined with comfort), and your elbows should be bent, not locked and stretched. Longer

and lower is faster; higher and shorter is more comfortable. Downhillers go with a shorter and higher cockpit. Because factory dimensions are based on a male's longer torso, most stock bikes are spec'd with stems too long for women. When you're buying a bike, the shop should swap stems at no (or little) cost.

* **Handlebar width**. A bar as wide as your shoulders gives you a good balance between control at slow and high speeds. The narrower the bar, the quicker the steering; wider bars give more leverage for climbing and horsing over technical sections.

* **Grips**. Squishy grips that feel big in your palm are more fatiguing than smaller, harder grips. Seems crazy, but it's true.

Gear and Clothing without Fear and Loathing

Beyond the rapture of riding and exploring the earth and stuffing your friends in a sketchy corner, mountain biking is a great sport because the gear is cool. It looks cool, it feels cool to wear and use, the colors are pretty, and you can sink criminal amounts of cash into things no one but fanatics will notice. Perhaps not even them.

Some novice mountain bikers take a while to experience the inexorable urge to buy gear—or simply need time to hang around enough riders to hear the excuses that work on family and mates. For them, here's a budget-minded guide to getting into the sport.

Must Have

* **Helmet** ($40–$150). Coolness always counts, but a bucket-shaped helmet is downright humiliating. Get something racy, with lots of vents to prevent your brain from overheating, a visor for blocking brush and the sun, and full-

Mountain biking's must-haves—all you really need to keep rolling.

face coverage if you're exclusively a downhiller. Make certain the helmet has stickers with ANSI, SNELL, or ASTM certification, which guarantee its worthiness. The brim should ride on your forehead instead of up near your hairline. The front and back straps should meet just below your ear. The chin strap should not hang loose, but it shouldn't be too tight to fit a small finger under. If you can rock the helmet off your head sideways or wiggle it front and back it's not on right—adjust the straps or the padding inside, or try a different size or style helmet.

* **Pump** ($15–$40). This mini-pump attaches to your frame or fits in a pocket or seat bag. Flat tires are the most common mountain bike breakdown. No pump is the most common cause of long walks.
* **Spare tube** ($3–$7). No spare is the second most common cause of long walks.

* **Tire patch kit** ($3–$5). Try the new kind, which doesn't require any glue.
* **Mini-tool kit** ($20–$60). Whether you get an "all-in-one" tool that resembles a Swiss Army knife, or a compact kit, you should be able to carry allen (hex) wrenches, screwdrivers, box wrenches, a chain tool, and other goodies in a package about the size of a deck of cards.
* **Seat bag** ($15–$80). A place for your spare, patches, mini-tool, and a peanut butter sandwich. The price goes up with styling, size, and with features such as waterproofing and mesh pockets for holding wet stuff.
* **Water bottles** and **cages** ($20–$70 for a set of two bottles and two cages). Water is life. Dehydration feels like death.
* **Lube** ($3–$5 per bottle). Lube is cheaper than chains, cogs, chainrings, and all the other stuff you'll ruin if you ignore it.

To cruise in comfort, add
these simple items.

Good to Have

* **Shorts** ($20–$80). Cycling shorts have a padded crotch to cushion your nethers and prevent chafing. You pay more money for better ergonomics (seams that don't cut across the crotch, more panels for comfort and strength) or fashion. Baggies—shorts that look like casual wear but have cycling-specific liners—cost more. If you regularly do rides longer than 10 miles, you'll want shorts. Some shorts designed specifically for women have more padding than shorts made for men, an addition experienced riders sometimes find bulky and uncomfortable. Most important: Don't buy cheap shorts with an exposed seam in the crotch.

* **Shoes** ($40–$200). You can get by with running shoes, but once you switch to real bike shoes you'll never ride without them. Mountain biking shoes have soles stiff enough to transfer most of your energy to the pedals, yet enough flex for those times you're off the bike and pushing (or carrying). Get a model with a rip-away sole that lets you install cleats for clipless pedals. Make sure there are enough straps or lacing to keep the heel tight when you pedal. High-tops protect your ankles from flying debris.

* **Gloves** ($15–$70). It's not just to look moto—gloves pad your palms and give you a place to wipe your nose. (That's not a joke. The thumb-wipe is a hallowed part of cycling.) Gloves also save your palms when you do the over-the-bar skid. Full-finger, three-quarter coverage, knuckle-jobs—it's all personal style.

* **Valve adapter** (50 cents). This little gem screws onto your Presta valve to let it accept a Schrader pump—the kind most common in the States. This means you can fill up at a stranger's house or at a handy garage when you're lost.

When you get serious about having fun, spring for this gear.

Pretty Good to Have

* **Jersey** ($30–$80). Made with high-tech materials that wick away sweat, mountain bike jerseys are also cut to be comfortable when you're leaning forward on your bike—they're longer in back and don't stretch tight across the shoulders or bunch up and flap around to irritate your skin in other places. Jerseys are usually made with one to three pockets in back for convenient storage of bananas, spare tubes, and the car keys you lose once a year when you wreck.

* **Jacket** ($30–$150). A rain-resistant, wind-proof jacket that breathes (allows moisture to escape but not get in) will double your riding time and opportunities. Get one cut for cycling.

* **Eyewear** ($30–$180). Stylish and vision-saving, the best glasses not only prevent branches from plucking your eyeball, they come with interchangeable lenses that let you modulate your vision for all conditions. Make sure your glasses are impact resistant and admired by people who know about such things.

* **Tights** ($25–$80). With long leggings and a jacket you can face weather that once drove you to watch too much MTV. Don't buy the ultra-thick models unless you plan to ride only in arctic conditions, and make sure to get a pair with zippers at the ankles so you don't have to remove your shoes to strip off your pants after you heat up on a ride.

* **Water bladder/hydration pack** ($30–$100). The largest of these water-toting backpacks lets you carry 200 ounces of fluid—enough to hydrate a small desert town. Capacity is nice, but the real benefit is that you can sip without taking your hands off the bar.

* **Socks** ($9–$20). They're made for cycling, which means—um, they have logos of cool companies on the ankle.

* **Pedal wrench** ($7–$30). It's long (for the leverage you'll need) and makes you

look like you know what you're doing. (Remember: The pedals are threaded into the cranks in opposite directions—unscrew the right pedal counterclockwise, the left pedal clockwise.)

* **Box wrenches** ($30–$100 for a complete set). Once you begin dissecting your bike yourself, you'll need these. You also need allen wrenches, but it's easier to get by with the allen wrenches in your mini-tool. Or you can spring for a set of those for $20 to $40, too. A good, cheap alternative is a Y wrench, which usually has 4-, 5-, and 6-mm allens all on one tool, for about $7. You can operate on most parts of the bike with those three sizes.

* **Cable cutters** ($20–$60). Don't cut your cables with the sharp inner section of pliers—you'll crimp or fray the cable. Get a specialty tool if you'll be doing any cable or housing replacements. If you never cut anything but cable with it, it'll last a lifetime.

Stuff that Means You're Way, Way Too Much into the Sport for Outsiders to Understand

* **Lights** ($50–$300). Night riding is sensory deprived nirvana. There are never any crowds, either. If you can afford only one light, get a helmet-mounted spot so you can always see in the direction you're looking. With a bar-mounted light your vision is restricted to the bike's forward path—no looking around corners.

* **Heart-rate monitor** ($60–$250). A must-have for racing and training fanatics, which means it's a fringe item for the population at large. The expensive ones let you download your heart-rate log directly into your home computer for analysis and to add to your feelings of inadequacy.

* **Workstand** ($70–$250). If you tear into your bike on a weekly basis, you need stability and a place to hang greasy rags. The best models clamp to the top

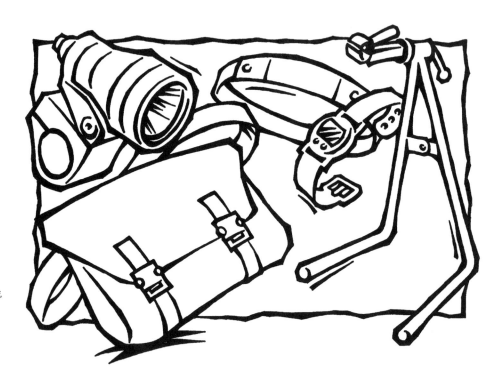

Once you "need" this stuff, you're lost in the sport. Congratulations!

tube or seat post rather than hooking onto the bottom bracket. Some stands fold for travel.

* **Backpack or messenger bag** ($50–$200). The hip way to haul. Cycling-specific backpacks have pockets for water bottles, a way to hook your helmet onto the outside, and a back support of mesh or other breathable material to keep you from getting all sweaty. I prefer messenger bags, which have a single strap that goes over one shoulder and crosses your chest. Riding high on your back, a messenger bag can hold anything and is timelessly hip and outlaw.

Pedal Principles

For safety, control, and efficient pedaling, it's important that your feet are *attached* to your pedals.

Plain cage pedals—with nothing to hold your foot—are the most dangerous kind of pedals to ride on. When the bike starts bouncing, your doggies slip off. This is bad. All of your weight plummets onto the saddle (or the top tube). Before that happens, though, your foot will probably wedge somewhere between the ground and the bike. That really hurts. You also don't get much power from your pedal strokes without attachment—there's no way to apply upward force—so you won't climb or cruise as well as you could if your feet were secured.

Some professional racers use plain pedals in dual-slalom competitions because, to cut tight corners at high speed, they need to slip one foot off the pedal and plant it as a pivot. But unless you wear a number plate on your back, stay away from pedals that don't secure your feet. Novice riders sometimes avoid toe clips or clipless pedals because they're afraid they won't be able to get their feet out of the pedals in time to avoid a wreck —but if you adjust the release system cor-

GO CLIPLESS, NOT TIPLESS

Here are seven tips for forging a loving relationship with clipless pedals:
* **Use a shoe with a stiff sole.**
* **Trim away shoe treads that interfere with the cleat/pedal interface.**
* **Clean the cleats and pedals regularly; use dry lube on the pedals' moving parts.**
* **Replace worn, ragged-edged cleats.**
* **Practice clicking out at all phases of the pedal stroke—not just at the bottom.**
* **Practice clicking in.**
* **If you fumble an entry, concentrate more on pedaling than clicking in. It's more important to maintain momentum than to engage your pedal.**

rectly there's nothing to worry about.

* **Clips and straps** (toe clips) bind your feet to the pedals. You slide your foot into a plastic or metal cage attached to the front of the pedal, then pull a strap tight across the top. To get out, you have to loosen the strap—so most beginners ride with the strap loose enough to let them pull both feet out instantly.

After several rides, try riding with one strap cinched tighter. You can do this before you start pedaling, but the pro way is to reach down with one hand and snug the strap while you coast. (You'll want your foot at the top of the pedal stroke for this, so make sure you're coasting on smooth ground—if the other pedal catches on an obstacle while you have one hand off the bar, there's gonna be trouble.) Once one foot feels comfortable strapped, try riding with both snug. In an emergency, when your body's pumping with adrenaline and hysteria, you can usually remove a foot by pulling back sharply—as if you're trying to scrape mud off your sole. The calm way to disengage is to coast, reach down, and flip the buckle to let slack into the strap.

* **Clipless pedals,** which look like little

platforms and engage a special cleat screwed into the sole of your shoe, are easier to get into and out of than clips and straps (especially when you're restarting on a trail, when the unoccupied toe clip inevitably flops to the underside of the pedal and drags along the ground). It just takes practice.

To Repair Is Human

My favorite philosophy of bike repair and maintenance was voiced by Steve Gravenites, a pro team mechanic known as Gravy. He's worked on more bikes than most of us will ever see, and the pros trust him with their paychecks. Gravy says, "Cleaning a bike's like cleaning a toilet. If you do it regularly, it's fine. If you wait, it's a truly disgusting experience."

I've stuck my hands in enough two-wheeled toilets to know that Gravy speaks the truth. Wash and lube your bike regularly, take it to a shop at the beginning and end of each season, and you'll save yourself much disgust.

Even so, your bike *will* break down on the trail. That's what mountain bikes do. Here's how to handle the five most common mechanical situations.

TRACTION TRICKS

For best traction and braking, make sure your tires are mounted with the treads facing forward on the front wheel and backward on the rear wheel. This setup maximizes traction in front and braking in back. Some tires have directional arrows printed on the sidewalls; others are made specifically for front or rear. Those are easy. If your tires have neither, look at the tread pattern: Toward the center of the tread there's usually a large V-shaped or pointed knob called a chevron—point the chevron forward for front and backward for back. If there's no chevron, look at the other treads: They usually slope on one end and cut off abruptly on the other—the slope is the front. Don't worry if you're stumped. Tires provide a little more control when they're pointed properly, but they work just fine even when oriented "wrong."

Fix a Flat

Deflate the tube completely. If you can't roll the tire off the rim with your hands (try it, because that's the coolest way), stick a pair of tire tools between the tire and the rim and flip the rubber off one side. Extract the tube. Carefully run your fingers along the inside of the tire to find the bad thing that caused the puncture. (If you don't, and the thorn or whatever is still in there, it'll rip open the replacement tube.)

Inflate the replacement tube just enough to make it round, slip it into the tire, and snap the tire back into the rim. The last few inches might be tough; push it on the rim with your thumbs if you can. If you can't, use the tire tools to pop it back on, but make sure you don't pinch the tube between the rim and the tool. Check to make sure the tire is seated in the rim all the way around—if it isn't, the tube will blow the tire off the rim when it's inflated. Inflate it halfway and check again. Then finish the job.

Lube Stuff

Your chain should be lubed before it gets dry and cleaned before it disappears behind its own grit. For some of us that's every ride; for others it's once a week. Clean the chain before you lube it, wiping it down with a rag soaked with liquid soap or a bike degreaser. (I like the citrus ones because they don't kill the earth and they smell dandy.) Simply hold the rag on the chain and backpedal 10 or 20 strokes. Then apply lube to each link. Let the lube sit for at least 10 minutes, then wipe the chain with a dry rag before you ride. This gives the lube time to penetrate into the links so you can remove it from the outside (where it does nothing but attract grime).

Your chain isn't the only thing that needs to be lubed regularly. Anything that moves on your bike needs help. That means cleat retention mechanisms in

After you remove the broken links, push the pin back in and finish your ride.

your pedals, brake pivots, cables, derailleur pivots, or anything that begins creaking.

Fix a Busted Chain

One day you'll hear a snap, then a demonic metal clatter, and then one of your knees will shoot forward and bang off the handlebar or stem. Your chain broke.

Don't panic. Stop, get off the bike, and look for the damaged link. Shift both derailleurs to their slackest positions, then derail the chain and sit it on the bottom bracket. (You do this to create some slack and make the chain easy to work with.)

Take your mini-tool out of your seat bag and use the chain tool to push out the pin holding the damaged link. Don't push the pin completely out or you'll never get it back in; just push it out enough so you can slip the bad link off.

Make sure you push out a pin that will let you match the broken chain ends—don't leave yourself a chain with two outer plates. (You'll need to remove one other link besides the broken one.) You need one inner plate and one outer plate to fuse the ends. This sounds confusing, but it's easy to see when you're staring at a broken chain. Work with the chain tool from the wheel side of the chain instead of facing the frame. You'll see why in a second.

Bring the ends together. Now, working from the outside—which is easier when you're trying to hold the ends of the chain together—use the tool to push the pin back in. You did it. If the link is tight, grab the links on either side of it and flex them laterally to loosen it. Now finish your ride. But remember: Your chain is two links shorter than it was a few minutes ago— be sure not to use gear combinations that stretch the chain.

Adjust Your Brakes

If your brakes suddenly seem slack after a long downhill, it probably doesn't mean you've worn out the pads to the point of replacement, which is what most novices assume. You've worn the pads, but you can usually get your braking back simply by dialing out the cable adjuster.

The whosit whatsit? The cable adjuster, also called a barrel adjuster, is a knurled, hollow screw that's found where the cable comes out of the brake lever. It's the only thing there that looks like a barrel, so you can't miss it. Dial the adjuster out, and it effectively lengthens the cable housing, which takes up some cable slack and brings your pads closer to the rim. (You'll look like a genius if you do this for someone who doesn't know what's happening.)

Adjust Your Shifting

When your lovable rig starts missing shifts or shifting on its own despite your most creative curses, it's time to adjust the shifter cable just as you did the brake cable. (Why? Cables stretch.) There are two barrel adjusters for the rear derailleur—one where the cable leaves the shift lever and one where the cable enters the derailleur. Dial either one *out* if you're having trouble shifting to big cogs, or *in* if you can't get to smaller cogs smoothly. The front shifting action can only be adjusted at the shifter. Adjusting the derailleur cables is harder to do right than a brake adjustment because the whole arrangement is more precise. Be patient and expect to make mistakes.

BECOMING AN EARTHSURFER: BASIC MOUNTAIN BIKING SKILLS

The guy on the bike in front of you careens to the right of the slat bridge that connects the foot-wide trail you're on with another one that looks even narrower, then he aims his bike into the mucky gash in the earth responsible for the bridge's existence.

Your best hope for your friend is that the freefall into the cravasse might coat his body with enough mud to keep his legs from snapping when he smacks back into the earth. But somehow the guy defies gravity and gets his bike to hop the gully. He lands in the middle of the narrow trail on the other side, remains upright, and begins scooting up an incline that would have given Sisyphus nightmares.

When that happened to me on my first ride, I simply stopped riding and stood in the middle of the trail, straddling my bike with the brakes clamped shut and my mouth stuck open. I knew I couldn't leap across that hole—let alone land safely and immediately climb the steepest hill I'd ever seen—if I practiced for the rest of my life. And yet I wanted to try it right away.

That's what it's like to be a beginner. Mountain biking will scare the hell out of you and seduce you at the same time. This feeling never goes away—not even for the pros—but novice riders tap into it more often and more intensely. In a way, there's no purer offroad riding experience than that of a beginner. Everything is fresh—and challenging. Every log is a triumph—or a disaster.

The beginner's learning curve is steeper than a World Cup downhill race course. You will never improve so much, so quickly. In some ways, riding will never be quite as fun afterward. (Though there's a lot to be said for knowing how to knife through a hairpin turn, maintaining your speed with a perfectly timed pedal kick, then launching off a rise at 30 mph, feeling the wind blow the good sense right out of your head. Being an expert is dandy, too.)

The First Fifteen Minutes

The first 15 minutes you spend on a mountain bike are the harshest. Even if you're on the flattest, widest trail in town you'll feel like you're threading the needle on a foot-wide singletrack of rocks and dirt at 10,000 feet in Crested Butte. I know, because I've been both places.

Don't let the vertigo discourage you. You will be unable to keep the bike on the trail. The damned thing will migrate to the edges of the singletrack or dirt road with unerring consistency. And the edges are where bad things happen—unseen dips suck your wheel down and out of your control; brush and branches reach out to grab your handlebar or wheel. You will feel things scratching your legs, and you probably will suffer through several awkward dismounts that dot your legs and arms with pretty, multicolored bruises. (Later you'll be proud of these, so don't get all out of whack.)

You might even wreck, and when it happens the contact points will be the ground and your face, your hands, your hips, or your shoulders. Don't worry about this too much, either. Everyone wrecks, and at beginner speed you're rarely going fast enough to damage anything except your enthusiasm. Maybe your ego, too.

On the rare moments when your body makes some kind of miraculous move you don't understand and you find yourself still on the trail, you will hit everything you can possibly hit. All of it—from the inch-high pebble to the snarling stream bed—will knock your wheels sideways with a force you have never felt before.

In my initial 15 minutes, on an eastern Pennsylvania trail I now consider easy, I tore my shiny new cycling shorts, sprained an ankle, and vowed to never ride on dirt again. I cursed my borrowed bike. I cursed wildflowers for blocking my view. And just what kind of idiot, I wanted to know, decided to run a trail right through the woods, anyway?

There's nothing you can do to avoid those 15 minutes. Your body needs time to adjust its vision, its balance, its coordination, and its thought processes to a strange world in which bikes go places that don't seem possible, where gravity (as well as the ground) feels a little funky. When whatever needs to click clicks (I distinctly remember such a sound at my moment of acclimation, although it might have been just another echo from that time my head dented a rock), your ride will settle into a smoother, faster rhythm. And you won't even know why.

Loose Rules

"You stopped riding like the Tinman," says my friend Dondo, who's been mountain biking just about since the modern ones were invented. He's slowed down to ride beside me on a section of doubletrack. "You're not as stiff." He takes one hand off the bar, reaches over and slaps my elbow. It swings an inch or so from side to side. "Still not right, but better than when we started."

He imitates my straight-armed, lock-legged first 15 minutes of mountain biking, and the difference is shocking. His upper body had been floating along beside me, calm and steady as his bike bucked beneath him on the trail. Now, the trail batters him completely. Every rock changes his line, angles his entire body up or down, pushes it to the side. He looks over at me to say visually, "See?" and rides right into a wheel-deep gully that stretches across the trail.

When we untangle ourselves from our bikes, he says, "So there's lesson one. A loose me would have gone right down and up that gully. And if you'd been loose enough you wouldn't have gone down when I fell on you."

Riding relaxed is one of the most important principles in mountain biking—just about every technique you'll learn is impossible if you remain stiff. (You'll never stop working on loosening up. At times even the greatest riders in the world struggle to stay relaxed—if that doesn't sound too Zen.)

Tense mountain bikers do a lot of things wrong. Their steering is unpredictable chickenscratch. They fatigue quickly and have little stability or control because every shock from the trail is transmitted from the bike through their stiff limbs.

When you relax, you flow.

RE: Relax

A tense mountain biker rides like an ice cube instead of like water. You want to flow, not bounce down the trail. The idea is to keep your upper body calm and steady while the bike bobs and swerves beneath you. If you can accomplish this you will have more stability and control. You'll also use less energy, and you'll be less likely to get hurt when you crash.

✳ **Hands:** You want a firm grip, but your hands should never *clench* the bar. Besides fatiguing your forearms, a death-grip makes your steering twitchy and over-responsive. Try keeping your fingers loose by occasionally drumming

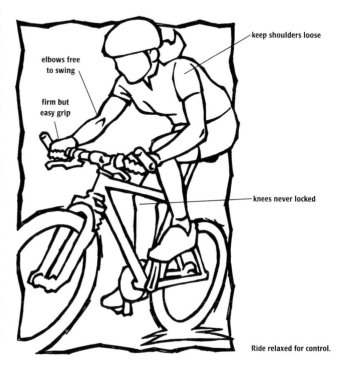

keep shoulders loose

elbows free to swing

firm but easy grip

knees never locked

Ride relaxed for control.

them against the bar, or imagine that your handlebar is twice as thick as it is.

* **Elbows:** Never lock your elbows. You want your arms to able to extend or compress instantly to absorb shock and keep you on a good line. If your elbows are rigid you cannot control your bike because you will be bouncing just as hard as it is. Practice swinging your elbows to keep them loose—make miniature flapping motions. It looks silly but it works.

* **Knees:** Your legs are the greatest suspension system your bike has. High-tech suspension forks get about three to four inches of travel; your legs can absorb two to three times that much—if you keep your knees loose. Novices tend to "brace" themselves against the trail by locking their legs. This is like riding on stilts instead of springs. Let your legs (like your arms) bend to absorb the jumps and jitters of the bike while your upper body stays steady.

* **Shoulders and jaw:** These don't have much to do with riding, but they're great indicators. If your shoulders are hunched or your jaw is clenched, chances are you're riding stiff.

Position of Power

You're almost ready to start learning some techniques. But first you need to understand one more thing about how to sit on your bike. (Relaxing is only the first half of the equation: It helps keep you on the trail, but it alone doesn't let you *respond* to the trail—you need to be able to spring forward, shift your weight around the bike, brake without unbalancing yourself, and absorb hits you never see.)

This is where mountain biking differs from other types of cycling you might have done. On a mountain bike, you need to get your body into a dynamic position that gives you complete control. This is called the *ready position*. It's the posture your body should assume whenever possible—when you're coasting, pedaling without having to juke over things, descending, and even between acrobatic moves. It's like a tennis player always returning to the baseline.

The basic idea is that you want to "float" over your bike rather than plant yourself on it. The greatest floater I've ever ridden with is a mountain biking legend named Don Cook. He used to race for one of the first pro mountain bike teams, then left that scene to help transform Crested Butte into a fat-tire Mecca, spending years finding and cutting many of the famous singletracks. Today he's a professional test rider—companies give him equipment so he can try to break it.

You're behind Cook on Snodgrass Trail, one of the easiest—but still fun—routes in Crested Butte. Watch how he hovers over his bike instead of driving it into the ground with his weight. When he turns, watch how his body leans out from his bike (an advanced skill we'll learn later), then snaps back to neutral position over the saddle. He's always centered. It's instinct—mountain biker's instinct.

Our traditional instinct is to sit firmly on the bike. Nothing could be worse on the trail. You must develop a mountain biker's instinct. Think about returning to the ready position. It won't feel natural at first. But after you master it you'll wonder how you ever rode any other way.

Ready for Action

The ready position gets its name because from it you can spring instantly into any of the actions you need to make your bike

riding relaxed

- **Grip the handlebar securely; never clench.**
- **Elbows loose, not locked.**
- **Flex your knees.**
- **Check your shoulders and jaw for signs of tension.**

flow or fly (or, in an emergency, stop). Here's the blueprint.

* **Elbows and knees flexed.** You're a boy, not a puppet, Pinocchio.

* **Cranks horizontal to the ground.** Keep your cranks at the 3 and 9 o'clock positions for two reasons. First, a low pedal will hang up on something protruding from the trail. (Worst case: broken foot or a spontaneous somersault into a patch of poison oak. Best case: severe wobbles and a bruise.) The second reason is to provide an even platform for your feet, which helps you use your legs to float around the bike.

    You also want to keep your "good foot" forward. This just means that you'll feel more comfortable and in control when a certain foot is forward or backward. Usually it's the same foot as your dominant hand, but not always. Experiment. (When you're tired on a long downhill where you've had your pedals level for some time, you might want to temporarily go "goofy foot"— put your non-dominant foot forward.)

* **Butt floating over the saddle.** When the trail is happening, mountain bikers rarely sit on their saddles. Instead, they kind of "float" their butts over it— lightly touching it but not putting much pressure down. In essence, you use the saddle more like a guide to locate the bike under you. If much of your weight is on the saddle, every time the rear wheel kicks it will kick you. If you're just grazing the saddle, when you feel it rise you'll know the bike is jumping and that it's time to absorb some impact. You'll also be able to flick your body around to maintain balance. If your butt is planted, first you have to unplant it before you can make a weight shift.

    You're searching for a fine line: You don't want to be so upright that most of your weight is on your feet—this will

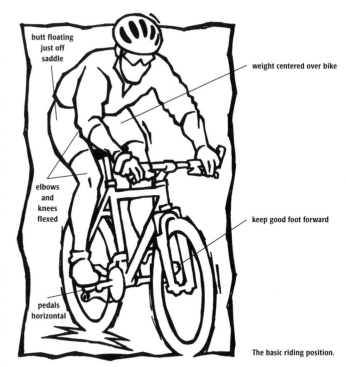

butt floating just off saddle

weight centered over bike

elbows and knees flexed

keep good foot forward

pedals horizontal

The basic riding position.

quickly tire your legs and will make your ride feel jerky. Any time you feel your body sticking onto one part of the bike, adjust. You want to distribute yourself so it feels like no part of the bike is bearing most of your weight.

Finding a Line

"Stop," says John Olsen as you begin to ride by him. John is a skills god, and when god speaks, you listen. You squeeze your brake levers. You get off your bike and stand beside him, waiting to see what will happen. You're in one of the ever-wet green forests in western Washington, on one of John's hometown trails. In this place, the good line is everything.

In many parts of the mountain biking world

get in the ready position

- **Flex your elbows and knees.**
- **Keep the cranks horizontal, with your most comfortable, "good foot" forward.**
- **Float just above the saddle.**

(perhaps where you live and ride) you can get by with a sloppy line—a path of travel that disrupts your bike's flow on the trail. A bad line costs you only some extra energy to oomph past it, or perhaps a mile per hour or two as your bike stutters. But out here, where John rides, it's the good line or no line, the perfect line or the painful limp.

"Close your eyes," says Olsen. "Now tell me what your line is for the next 30 feet."

When he did this to me, I couldn't describe my line for the next five feet. It was one of the reasons that, as John demonstrated, he could use the same basic moves I did but ride farther than I could. He knew how to pick a line.

It's a tough skill to master, one that you'll keep learning well into the intermediate stage, and one that you'll refine every time you ride a new type of terrain. But it's also one of the most natural skills to develop. Once you understand the basic

principles you'll keep improving as long as you keep riding.

A good line isn't always the smoothest or the shortest. It's the one that keeps your bike moving the fastest with the least amount of energy expended. To see these lines you need to develop mountain biking vision: You need to learn to scan the entire trail but concentrate only on the parts that will affect your progress.

When you begin picking lines, you will probably think of them as smooth or bumpy, clean or littered. You'll know you're getting the skill when you start identifying lines as rideable, rideable faster, or not rideable. Then you're looking at the line, not the things lying over (or under) it.

Eye Do

If you ride long enough you'll develop the ability to pick out the best line for your bike (and you) to travel. But you don't have to wait—you can train your eyes to view the world through dirt-colored goggles. Here's how.

look where you want to go, instead of at what you want to miss

Picking a line.

* **Look where you want to go—don't stare at what you want to miss.** Your bike will follow your vision. Fixate on that tombstone rock and you'll plow into it; get captivated by that ditch and you'll kiss its mucky bottom. So scan the entire trail, focus on obstacles just long enough to let them register in your brain, then aim your sight to the clear path you want to follow.

* **Look ahead—don't look down at your wheel.** By the time you see objects immediately ahead, you won't be able to react to them. In typical conditions, try aiming your vision 30 to 40 feet down the trail. (Adjust this to conditions—as little as 5 or 10 feet on slow, technical trails, as much as 100 feet or more on fast, open rides.) Trust your organic computer to plot a course and to communicate the coordinates with your body. As you look ahead, your

freaky subconscious will ride things you cannot see. Pretty cool.

* **Scope it all—don't just look at rocks and logs.** Keep your head moving and note as much as you can. Is the trail surface wet or dry? Where it cuts sideways into the incline, does it angle into the hill or away from it? Is there room on the side to biff safely if you blow it? Is the bend in the trail ahead going to take you back across the stream you just came through?

* **Take the wrong line sometimes.** Try a path you consider foolish or impossible. See what happens if you crank over a rock bed instead of opting for the wet sand beside it. As a novice, it's more important to build a repertoire of line knowledge than to always stay safe. Sometimes a bad line can teach you more about a good line than a good line can. Got that?

Braking News

You shuttled the first three uphill miles in one of the guide's trucks, then pedaled another three up a gradually inclining mix of trails and abandoned roads before popping into the sun on a low-lying crest in Washington's Cascade Mountains. You stop, drink some water, look at the single-track that squiggles its brown line across the green field before falling away into blue sky.

You wonder what you're doing in this group—two professional guides, a veteran of the Iditabike race in Alaska, a wiry aerobic animal who climbs like a Jeep, and you. And then you're following them, punching gears and carving, surfing, floating, out of your mind and out of your body with the effort to stay with them, but staying with them.

The group stops for a water break and everyone just laughs. No need for talk on a ride like this. Then you're all sprinting down a logging road, spinning out your biggest gears and threading through each other's lines in corners. "I'm maxing at 53," yells someone with a speedo.

How would you handle a rut at that speed? Here's what not to do: Stick your front wheel in and brake hard. My shoulder still makes noises from that wreck.

spot a good line

- Look where you want to go, not at what you want to miss.
- Look ahead, not directly in front of your wheel.
- Look at all the trail features.
- Take a bad line sometimes to learn more.

Brakes and Breaks

I snapped my clavicle on Buck Mountain because I braked too hard—a common mistake that costs a lot of beginners important pieces of their body. *Modulated braking*—a controlled application of just enough force to slow you—is the main braking skill you should focus on.

But braking, like mountain biking, is not just about avoiding injury. There's also euphoria to chase. Experienced riders tap into a ride's rhythm. They swoop and flow along trails, pulled by a current that unravels the miles instead of piling them on. Novices rarely feel this because their clumsy braking disrupts the rhythm. Beginners tend to use brakes too hard and too often.

If you trust your braking ability you'll ride safer. But you'll also ride better.

Slowing to Perfection

The first step to heavenly braking is knowing which lever controls which wheel. Too basic? Not really. You probably already know your right lever operates the rear brake (remember: R = R), and your left controls the front. But you need to absorb this information until it exists at the level of instinct. When you brake in a panic you don't want to mistakenly mash the front lever.

Your leading brake has so much stopping power that it can instantly freeze your bike, whipping you over the handle-

Shift Happens

One of the most embarrassing things to admit is that you don't understand shifting. No big deal. I didn't when I began riding, and neither did anyone else. Here's everything you need to know but can't ask anyone.

* Your *right* shifter operates the *rear* derailleur. That's easy to remember: R = R.

* In front, when you shift to a smaller chainring (mountain bikes have three) it makes the pedaling easier. When you're on terrain that increases your rolling resistance (a hill or deep mud), you want easy pedaling—so you should go to the small or middle chainring. Use the big ring only when you're smoking. When I was a novice, most of my riding was on the small ring. Now I do a lot of middle-ring riding.

* In back, when you shift to a smaller cog (mountain bikes have seven to nine cogs) it makes pedaling harder. So for tough terrain you want to be on a big cog.

* Front and rear shifting work in combination. The easiest gear is small ring in front/big cog in back. The hardest gear is big ring in front/small cog in back. All the other combinations are somewhere between these two efforts.

* Never put the chain on big ring/big cog or small ring/small cog. This runs the chain at a severe angle that wears your equipment faster, makes the chain more likely to jump loose, or may even trash your derailleurs.

* When expert dirt riders start slinging lingo like "shift up" or "higher gear," don't get confused. Use the H-rule to figure out what they're talking about. Higher means harder gears. Remember that things go up to go higher—so *shift up* means a *higher* (harder) gear.

* Try to find a good gear with the rear shifter first. If you can't, shift in front to find a whole new range. With experience you'll know when to shift the front without trying all the gears in back.

* Generally you want to be in a gear that allows you to spin between 60 and 85 to 90 rpm. This is the best range for efficient pedaling (your body doesn't use too much energy) and to avoid straining your knees or leg muscles. You won't maintain this rate on most hills unless you're a pro, though. Don't sweat it. Just find the most comfortable cadence.

* If all this is overwhelming, shift onto the small ring in front, then adjust only the rear gear during your rides. This limited range will allow you to climb hills and cruise on rolling ground, though you won't attain maximum speeds. But that's okay until you're ready to add the front gears to your repertoire.

* Anticipate shifts. Shift down before a climb, up before you drop into a descent. Some cheap shifting systems won't change gears under pressure, so by the time you're straining up the hill you're stuck in a too-high gear. But more important: Good shifting is good rhythm. You want your bike to glide and swoop, not stall and recover.

* Shift more than you think you should. Beginners never shift enough—they try to tough out a slightly mismatched gear. Watch the good riders: They fine-tune their gearing to the terrain. One click makes a big difference.

bar. (Most of us discover this at some point early in our riding lives.) This much power is a good thing—if you know how to harness it. But some novices are so freaked out by the mighty front brake that they ignore it completely. This is like pedaling with one leg.

You can master the front brake with a grassy-field drill. At a walking pace, clamp down on the left lever. Your rear wheel will jump off the ground. Stay calm, let go of the lever, and you'll return to the ground. (If your wheel didn't rise, brake harder next time.) Now do the same thing, but this time move your body weight backward as you brake. As you move farther back, more braking force is required to up-end the bike.

Got that? Now here's how a typical braking sequence should go: With two fingers on each brake lever, apply both brakes at the same time, with slightly more pressure on the rear than on the front, then gradually increase the force on the front brake. As you do this, gently shift some of your body weight back on the saddle. If your rear wheels starts to skid, apply more front brake; if your front wheel skids, modulate the lever until the skidding stops.

Funky Conditions and Finger Position

It's important to adapt the basic braking sequence to changes in terrain. In mushy stuff like sand, gravel, or mud, your front wheel tries to dig in or dive away from you. So use as much rear as possible, or try to scrub off your speed before you enter a messy section. A good rule: Brake hard when the ground is hard; brake soft when the ground is soft.

Braking in corners is bad for beginners. If you try to reduce speed after your bike has begun its lean or when your front wheel is angled, you'll wreck. Expert riders brake late in corners or use the rear brake to fling their bikes around. Don't try it yet. Slow to a safe speed before you

Apply both brakes at once, with slightly more pressure on the rear before gradually increasing the force in front.

Two fingers on the lever is normal. Add or subtract one to vary your braking power.

Control your braking force by varying the number of fingers on the lever.

If you try to brake in a turn, your wheels wash out.

how to brake

- Know which brake is which: **Right is for the rear wheel—R = R.**
- Use two fingers on each lever.
- Apply both brakes at once, with slightly more pressure on the rear.
- Gradually increase force on the front brake; shift your body weight back.
- If the rear wheel skids, release the lever slightly and apply more front brake (move your body weight back as you apply more force in front).
- If the front wheel skids, release the lever until the wheel rolls freely.
- Brake hard when the ground is hard, soft when the ground is soft.
- Brake *before* corners.
- Control braking force by varying the number of fingers on the lever.

enter a turn, or else just hang onto the grips and try to ride out the curve.

Braking technique also changes on downhills (that's explained in the section on descending), but the principle is similar: As you brake in front, move weight back; when the rear wheel skids, use more front.

A cool way to control your braking power is to adjust how many fingers you pull the lever with. Normal conditions: two. Soft and fuzzy: one front, two or three in back. Downhills: two in front, two in back. Long, steep downhills: three in front (to prevent fatigue), one in back (to prevent skidding).

Get Over It

You thought your friends asked you to go mountain biking, but you're spending most of your time mountain hiking—pushing, pulling, toting, and tossing your bike. Unlike the smooth trails you've ridden before, this one is rooted and rutted, littered with branches and rocks and sometimes whole trees.

The riders in front of you climb—or leap—everything. You tried. You plowed into a log and your bike slammed to a stop before your body did. (Your stomach still hurts where the stem punched it.) When you ran into a rock half the height of your hub, your front wheel turned sideways and pitched you off the bike. (So much for that new jersey.) You got your front wheel over that small tree back around the corner, but the rear wheel hung up and stalled you out, tipping you into a particularly impressive slow-motion free fall, first to the tree, then, after a bounce, to the soil.

That was the indignity—and the budding scar—that convinced me I needed heels instead of wheels to get over bumps. I walked everything on that ride through tough Eastern singletrack—even stuff less than six inches high, stuff the other riders were simply rolling over without fancy hops or wheelies. It was the closest I've ever come to quitting.

I think this is because getting over things is one of the essences at the cool center of the soul of our sport. If you don't have this bit of mountain bikeness down deep inside, all your riding will be somewhat hollow. There must be something to this theory because, completely apart from peer pressure, failure to scale things shreds your esteem at a level usually reserved for stuff like not finding dates or jobs or friends. It hurts way more than it should.

The secret to rolling over things is that you can't just roll over them. Even two-inch-high obstacles require a choreogra-phy of weight shifts and momentum that, once learned, seems simple. It's that once-learned part that messes us up so much in the beginning.

But within minutes of trying these techniques—and I've seen it happen to hundreds of riders when I teach clinics—you should be riding over objects as high as six or eight inches.

To go higher you learn how to *wheelie*, the easiest technique for getting over things up to a foot high. Higher than that you get into bunny hops, chainring grinds and other radical tricks. But even with those funky aerial maneuvers the basis will be the six simple steps that first help you roll over twigs and pebbles.

On a Roll

With this process I've coaxed first-time mountain bikers—people who still aren't even sure how to shift—over railroad ties, parking blocks, and, occasionally with a particularly errant novice, my feet. Practice on something under five inches high until you feel confident—then you should be able to use the same movements to clear obstacles up to eight inches high.

* **Approach with enough speed.** If you're going too slow, the bike simply halts when it hits an object, or else it loses so much momentum that it stalls halfway over. You want to approach with enough speed so that even if you didn't pedal for two feet before the collision you would still clear the obstacle. This will feel way too fast for you, but it's right.

* **Hands off the front brake lever.** I always keep two fingers on the brake levers—it's a good habit that will save your butt someday when you need a reflexive emergency stop, and it keeps your hands in position to feather the brakes to gracefully modulate speed—but when I learned to roll over things I had to take my fingers off the front lever because I kept panicking in mid-

 how to roll over things

- Approach with enough momentum to prevent stalling.
- Remove your fingers from the front brake lever.
- Unweight the front wheel by shifting your body slightly rearward.
- Absorb the impact with your elbows and knees.
- When your front wheel hits ground on the other side of the object, help push the bike over by returning your arms to their normal position.
- Shift your weight forward—back into the ready position—to unweight the rear wheel as it crosses the object.

To roll over a log, shift your weight back and absorb the impact by bending your arms and legs.

rollover and jamming the brake. I did a lot of handlebar flips because of that.

* **Get into the ready position.** We've already talked about how you should hold yourself on the mountain bike. Rolling over things is one of those times when you'll understand why it's important to ride with your elbows and knees flexed, your cranks horizontal, and your butt floating above the saddle.

* **Unweight the front wheel while holding it steady.** Shift your body slightly rearward from the ready position. Your weight will be off the front. Don't shift too far back—a few inches is usually enough. You're doing it right when your elbows are a little more than

halfway between a 90-degree bend and a straight-armed position. And keep those joints loose—you'll find out why later.

Steadiness is important, too. Imagine you're jogging and you run into a brick wall. It's easier to turn and run alongside the wall than to climb it. This is how your front wheel behaves. Unless you force it to climb, it will turn. Grip the handlebar firmly and counter-steer against the wheel's twitches. It'll take a while to find the compromise between unweighting the wheel and keeping control, but you'll get there. Took me ten attempts to nail the position.

* **Absorb the impact with your elbows and knees.** When the front wheel hits, let the bike come up toward your chest. Your elbows, which were partially extended, will bend as this happens. They're acting as shock absorbers to keep the bike from sticking on the object. Your knees play a similar role, but it happens more naturally than with the elbows. I never had to worry about the knees. Stiff arms were my source of faceplants (wrecks where you fly over the handlebar and land on your face).
* **Return your arms to their original position** when your front wheel hits the ground on the other side. This pushes the bike away from you (forward) and helps bring the rear wheel over.
* **Return to the ready position while unweighting the rear wheel.** Shift your weight forward, returning to your natural stance. This happens automatically—except for the first few times when you're so scared you've stiffened your arms and have a deathgrip on the handlebar.

Wheelie Flying

You use the same back-and-forth motion to get over things taller than eight inches, but your front wheel will need help climbing the obstacle. Learning to raise the wheel depends more on timing than strength—you don't so much *pull* the front of your bike up as you *pop* it up.

The techniques for doing this are the same ones that will some day let you pull a cool, styling, giddyup rolling wheelie in front of your admiring neighbors. But for now you don't have to scrape your head

To wheelie, first compress the front wheel, then lift back and up.

against clouds or ride one-wheeled 50 feet to be effective. You just have to get the front wheel off the ground about four inches or so.

- **First, do the cheater's wheelie.** Approach in the ready position and unweight before impact (just as you do when you want to roll over something). But this time, flap your arms backwards. To picture this movement, tuck your hands into your armpits and try to fly. Now flap in the other direction. That's it. This pulls the front end toward you (up and back, toward your chest). The combination of your pull and the obstacle's push will raise your front wheel just enough to help it roll up the object instead of butting against it. Cool and simple, huh?
- **Now the real thing.** Press down on the handlebar before you unweight the front. This compresses the front wheel, so when you shift your weight back the wheel rebounds and raises itself off the ground. When this happens, do the reverse flap. The wheel will rise higher. It's like combining two small wheelies into a larger one.
- **Try a power stroke.** To gain even more vertical, mash the pedal down with your dominant foot just as you flap. This adds so much force you might flip the bike backwards the first time you try it, so be careful.
- **Finesse the landing.** Getting back to the ground involves the basic forward shift back into the ready position (the move that helps you unweight the rear wheel when you're rolling over objects), but after a wheelie you come off obstacles at more extreme angles. It's easy to shift too far forward and flip over the handlebar in an endo. To save yourself, find a balance point where your body is still back but not over the rear wheel. I concentrate my mass over the bottom bracket.

Get a Grip

"You do not love your handlebar," says Dondo, who was one of my riding mentors when I was just starting. He's stopped right in the middle of a grooving ride around Blue Marsh Lake, one of the rare East Coast singletracks that's as smooth as anything west of the Rockies. We were snaking along the trail, stupid and happy with the simple pleasure of uncluttered fast riding under an early fall sun.

What he's said is true (I love few inanimate things), but it hardly seems worth the interruption. Until he turns it into a skills lesson.

WHAT'S WRONG WITH YOUR WHEELIE?

Here are five goofs novices just love to make, plus five fixes you'll love making even more.

- **Starting the wheelie too soon or too late.** Yowie. Bouncy, bouncy, ooey. If the wheel is falling on the object, begin later; if it's running into the object, start sooner.
- **Not compressing the wheel enough.** If the first part of your two-part wheelie isn't happening, try pressing down longer instead of harder. For some reason this works.
- **Not shifting your weight back.** In my first few attempts I squashed the front tire correctly but didn't move backward. I was trying to do all the work with my arm flap. But pulling the handlebar accomplishes nada if your weight is sitting on the front wheel. You can't lift yourself, or some such law of physics.
- **Mis-timing the flap.** If you never wheelie more than three or four inches you aren't pulling the wheel higher after the initial compression. You're probably flapping too soon. Let the wheel rise to the top of its compression flight before you flap.
- **Letting your front get your rear in trouble.** After I learned to loft my front wheel I found I could get it over foot-high obstacles—but then I had no idea how to get the rest of the bike to safety. Your wheelie ability will develop quicker than the other skills needed to cross way-high stuff. Use that thing called common sense.

doing a wheelie

- First learn the simple version: Unweight before impact and flap your arms backward.
- For additional loft, press down on the handlebar to compress the front wheel before you unweight it.
- Pull the front up farther with your arms by doing the reverse flap.
- Give a hard power stroke with your dominant foot just as you flap.
- Shift your weight forward to unweight the rear wheel and return to the ready position.

"When you love someone you know how to hold hands," Dondo says. "You know just where to interlace your fingers and how to make the hold soft but secure. And your hand never gets cramped or achy because you find just the right angle. *You* don't love your handlebar."

None of us does when we begin riding. We clench the grips, letting shock run up through our arms until we're fatigued and out of control. But that's only the most obvious mistake. Novices also hold one hand position too long, and they align their wrists and forearms in a way that leads to awkward handling and less security.

Grip Session

I know what you're thinking. *Grip? Grip?* You're doing everything you can just to stay on the trail and keep skin on your legs—can't a small subject like grip wait?

Nope. Your hands are one of the key connectors between you and your bike—a pathway for transmitting your skills into the front of the bike. Those mitts are also like your back—when fatigue hits them,

your whole body feels whipped. You're wasting yourself when you still have energy left to burn.

If your wrists and fingers ache after a ride, you don't love your handlebar. Spend some time perfecting your grip, and you'll not only ride longer with less fatigue, but other riding skills will be easier to enact.

* **Use the pro position.** All good riders use the same grip, which is no accident. Your wrist and forearm should be aligned—no bend between them—and angled slightly down. If your hands are horizontal, you're dropping your wrists and creating a bend that decreases control and increases fatigue. It also makes the reach to the brake lever longer, which wears out your fingers.

* **On descents, maintain the basic position but rotate your hands slightly forward**—no more than a quarter inch. This gives you better control of the front wheel and lets you work the brake levers for extended periods without excess fatigue.

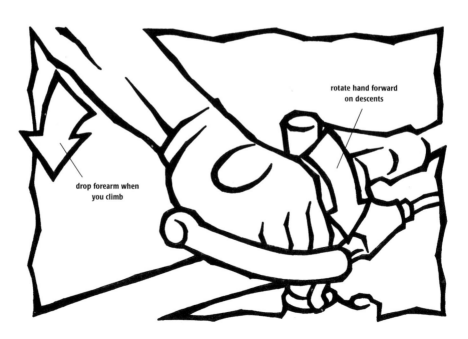

rotate hand forward
on descents

drop forearm when
you climb

Basic grip position.

* **On ascents, your grip should include a bend**—drop your forearms and straighten your wrists. This helps you maintain traction because you're weighting the front wheel more but also directing some force into the back wheel.

Going Up

"Descending is cool, but climbing is truth," says Scot Nicol. He's the creator of Ibis bikes (among the most beautiful and railed in the world), a former trials competitor, a thoroughly honed rider, and one of those guys who, in the middle of an epic ride, comes up with a single sentence that helps you realize more about mountain biking than you'd absorb in an hour-long clinic.

Scot is also the rider who's been half a wheel in front of you for the past half hour, cajoling you up a Colorado climb that started at 10,000 feet on a dirt road, and now, on singletrack around 11,000 feet, is as ragged as the breaths you're sucking. Suddenly, without showing any more effort, he pulls away from you and powers across the 50-yard gap to the lead group. When he reaches the pack he pops a wheelie and rides it for 10 seconds across slanted terrain you know you'll barely be able to pedal on.

Climbing is truth. Nothing makes you feel more like a beginner than sucking wind while others rage. Or when your rear wheel decides to retract its claws and spin out instead of gripping dirt. The difference between you the beginner and that lead group is partly fitness and partly technique.

Fitness takes time—it will come naturally if you keep riding. Technique takes work—but you can amp up your climbing skill immediately. This is because novices commit vital errors when they climb, mistakes you can fix on your very next ride.

Once you understand how to position yourself for maximum efficiency and traction, how to pick a good climbing line, when you should climb while seated and when you should stand, you'll be on your way to catching that lead group. These skills form the foundation that other ascending tricks are built on. Later you'll learn how to climb faster and smarter, and how to pop over obstacles uphill. But now your focus should be on developing a smooth climbing style.

Climb Time

It's okay if you hate climbing. Lots of people do. It's not okay if you never become good at it (which, unfortunately, lots of people also do). There's a sick satisfaction that comes with cleaning a tough climb. And there's a big reward for learning to ascend: descending. Here's how to claim bigger and bigger rewards.

* **Climb like a climber.** Just as we learned a standard position for cruising (cranks level, weight slightly off the saddle, elbows and knees loose), there's a climbing stance that's most effective for most situations.

    Flex your elbows and bend forward at the hips, keeping your back straight. You should be leaning toward the handlebar and your butt should be pushed back on the saddle a bit. This lowers your center of gravity, distributes your weight, and allows you to easily make the weight shifts and movements you'll need to maintain traction and power. Novices usually don't bend toward the bar enough. If you want to go up, you have to get down. On a simple climb, I usually have my nose 13 to 15 inches above the stem.

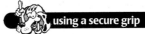
using a secure grip

- **Align wrists and forearms—no bend— and angle slightly downward.**
- **Descents: Rotate your hands slightly forward.**
- **Ascents: Drop your forearms and hold your wrists closer to horizontal.**

- Get into the climbing position.
- If the grade steepens, maintain front traction by dropping closer to the bar.
- If the back wheel begins to lose traction, decrease your amount of lean toward the handlebar.
- Relax.
- On smooth ascents, place your hands lightly on handlebar near the stem.

✸ **Maintain traction.** You do this by modifying your standard climbing position. As the pitch steepens, lean more toward the bar (drop your nose closer). This puts more of your weight over the front and, at the same time, pushes your butt back to keep weight over the rear tire.

You need to tune yourself until you find the angle of lean that keeps both wheels rooted. (Front wheel loose: too little lean; back wheel loose: too much.) At first you'll overshoot the sweet spot both ways before dialing in. The adjustments are more subtle than you expect.

✸ **Relax.** Of course. As always. Et cetera. Like so much of mountain biking, staying loose is one of the best things you can do. It conserves energy, and if you're not riding tight you're less likely to lose control when you roll through loose sections or over obstacles. Concentrate on keeping your upper body loose. Think about not clenching your shoulders. And remember, your jaw and hands also are good indicators—if they're tight, the rest of your body probably is, too.

On a smooth, moderately steep ascent, you can even take your hands off the grips or bar ends and lay them lightly on the bare handlebar between the grips and stem. Drum your fingers to keep them loose; keep just enough pressure on the bar to guide yourself.

Does Standing Deliver?

Most mountain bikers do most of their climbing in the saddle. Standing feels powerful, but when you rise out of the saddle you use about 12 percent more oxygen and raise your heart rate about 8 percent, or so the lab geeks say. Whatever

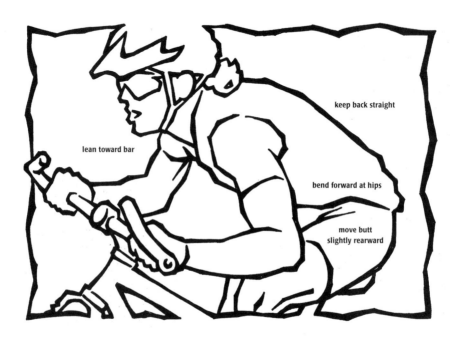

keep back straight

lean toward bar

bend forward at hips

move butt slightly rearward

Climbing with control.

the numbers, there's no doubt that standing is harder on your body. It requires more effort because your legs must both provide locomotion and support your weight.

But if you never stand to climb, you're ignoring one of your most valuable skills. Done properly, standing lets you deliver more power to the pedals while delaying fatigue by using muscles differently. It also lets you stretch during extended climbs.

As with most things mountain bike, there are no rules dictating how often and how long you should stand. Just some good generalizations.

* Most heavy riders do better when they climb seated more often than they climb standing; the opposite applies to light riders.

* If you use a suspension fork, stay in the saddle as much as possible. (The power thrusts of standing and pedaling can make the fork bob and waste energy.)

* Most novices don't stand often enough—and when they do they stand for too long.

Understand the Stand

Remember, you don't jump out of the saddle on a climb just because it looks cool (though, heck, it does look really cool)—you do it to change positions and give your aching body a break, to muscle through a tough section, or for an added power boost when your grandma's threatening to take you at the crest. Here's the lowdown on getting up.

keep lower back straight

sway your bike from side to side in time with pedal strokes

scoop pedals back and up

Get out of the saddle to surge uphill.

* As your foot begins a downstroke, shift to a harder gear (if you don't, you waste energy with loose, sloppy pedal strokes), then rise out of the saddle. If you have bar ends, move your hands out to them. You should be as upright as the pitch of the hill will allow, with your chest out over the handlebar. Your lower back should be straight. Sway

climbing out of the saddle

- If you have bar ends, move your hands out to them.
- Shift to a harder gear and rise out of the saddle.
- Be as upright as the pitch allows.
- Keep your back straight.
- Sway the bike from side to side in time with each pedal stroke.
- "Scoop" the pedals backward and up on each stroke.
- Return to the saddle when the grade lessens; shift back to an easier gear.

Save energy by climbing the longer—but shallower—line.

the bike from side to side (but no more than a foot each way)—this establishes a rhythm and makes your downstrokes more direct and powerful. (Some riders like to pull up on the bar while pushing down with their legs. I push because I can do so without clenching my hands.)

* You're doing it right when you realize why good riders describe standing as "running on the pedals." If you feel jerky and uncontrolled, you're either not pushing a big enough gear or you're completely straightening your leg on the downstroke. Go for a 95 percent bend and concentrate on "scooping" your pedals backward and up. This eliminates the dead spot at the bottom of a stroke.

climbing tactics

- If you have a low enough gear, spin the pedals at 60 to 70 rpm for efficiency.
- Ride the shallower outside line on uphill curves.
- Ride straight; don't weave.
- Use the bar ends even if you aren't standing.

* Don't sit back down when the grade is steep—you'll stall. Wait for a flatter section. If you can't find one, you shouldn't have stood. You just learned something. Cool, huh? Remember to shift back to an easy gear as you return to the saddle.

More Upward Mobility

Besides the basics, there are a few easy-to-use tricks that help you make the instant transformation from clueless climber to not bad.

* **Spin if you can.** When possible, shift to a gear low enough to let you spin the pedals about 60 to 75 rpm. When your cadence is slower than this, your heart rate, energy use, and perceived exertion increase. This will happen to you. A lot. Don't worry about it. That's one of the reasons climbing sucks.

* **Ride the outside line on curves.** You have a choice when riding around an ascending curve. The inside line is shorter, but steeper and harder. As you go farther outside, the pitch usually becomes shallower. If the terrain is equally smooth on both lines, ride the outside one. The extra distance doesn't hurt as much as the extra grade.

* **Ride straight.** Weaving is for wussies. Even changing your steering angle by a single degree increases rolling resistance about 6 percent; a 3-degree variation raises it 30 percent. Riding straight feels like it hurts more, but it doesn't.

* **Use your bar ends even when you aren't standing.** It wastes energy, but there's nothing like grabbing those babies and pumping the bike up a steep section. You get way more leverage when your hands are farther apart. But you should also stick your hands on the bar ends even when you don't need to crank the bike from side to side: The wider position opens your chest and lets you breathe easier.

Restarting on a Climb

Blowing up on a climb isn't so bad—it's when you can't get on your bike and ride again that true misery sets in. Walking sucks. The problem most novices have is that when they begin pedaling uphill from a standstill they cannot gain momentum and keep traction at the same time. So something gives. That something is you. Here's how to restart.

* Angle your bike to point across the trail instead of straight uphill. The angle should be gentle—just barely off line (though still facing uphill), not perpendicular to the trail.

* Seat yourself on your bike with your foot engaged in the downhill pedal. (This will be the one highest from the ground because of the slope.) Your other foot can easily reach the ground to support you.

ROLLERS AND REAL CLIMBS

A climb is any ascent long enough to make you regret being on it. A roller is a short, severe rise that's usually too steep to pedal over with good traction. You can't use traditional climbing techniques on a roller because your wheels won't bite or the angle is too sharp to make pedaling practical. The idea is, simply, to approach the roller with enough speed to coast to the crest. Remember to keep your cranks level, or they'll hang up on the peak. Once you've topped out, push the handlebar down the other side by extending your elbows. This keeps your bike from hanging up on the crest. You can also kick the bike over by doing a quick half-stroke to maintain momentum, then leveling the pedals again.

Once you understand the rhythm, rollers are fun. With practice, you can handle rollers higher than your head.

You can restart on any hill. Angle bike across trail, then up; keep foot at two o'clock for short but powerful stroke; and push off with loose foot.

Work your bike for extra speed on rollers. At the crest, push bar down and forward; level your pedals for clearance.

✸ Move the pedal that has your foot in it to either the 10 or 2 o'clock position (depending on the side of the bike). From here you'll be able to give a quick but powerful downstroke.

✸ As you give the downstroke, push off slightly with your free foot.

✸ Once you feel the slightest surge of power, turn your bike straight up the hill. Don't wait too long and ride off the trail or make the turn so sharp that you lose your momentum or balance.

✸ Don't worry about clicking your free foot in until your pace is steady and sure. Until then, just rest your foot on top of the pedal.

The Decent Descent

You stop. You look over the edge. The earth plunges away from your feet at an angle you couldn't safely walk down. Somewhere below—beyond the lip of the drop-in, past the half-buried boulder you'll have to pray for otherworldly traction to traverse, through that jagged rut and then around the hairpin where the angle of the trail's descent seems to become even sicker—somewhere down there are your friends. Waiting for you. Waiting to laugh at you. When you walk. Again.

You know your brakes can't overcome the gravity of this situation—on a pitch like this the most they can do is reduce acceleration. And there's no bailing—no way to put a foot down on this baby. You commit or walk. You commit to the stupid, wonderful, insane joy that is descending, or you walk.

I committed. I shredded the edge of my adrenaline for 20 glorious seconds, and then I shredded the skin off my legs and arms for what felt like another 20 but was actually perhaps 5.

The dirt tasted bitter, and the flayed parts of my body screamed at me. But I wanted more of those 20 seconds; I wanted that feeling of *surfing the earth*. That was when I became a downhiller.

I had all kinds of lessons to learn, and some of them I'm still trying to master today—as all mountain bikers are, whatever their skill level. But that moment when I stopped regarding descents with only fear—and instead began drinking the tasty mix of fear and awe that pours down hills—that was when I became a downhill mountain biker.

Some of you are like this from the first ride; some of you might take months, or even years, to become intoxicated with downhilling. The pace doesn't matter. What's important is keeping your body more or less together (you will tear it up a little) so you can enjoy downhilling.

I learned the stupid way—the collarbone-busting, skin-grating, muscle-ripping method. There's a better course. All you need is a short (less than 30 seconds to descend at walking pace), moderately steep, smooth downhill—your practice hill.

You will love this hill (even if you hate it at first) because at slow speeds you'll learn the fundamentals of descending: Approach at a comfortable pace, set up your body to maximize control, shift your weight back just the right amount to coordinate your center of gravity to the pitch, brake strongly without skidding or flipping over the handlebar, and exit with grace and momentum.

These skills work for any pitch at any speed. Absorb them in safety—the way I wish I'd done it—and you'll never fear

safe descending

- Shift to a gear combination that keeps your chain taut.
- Level the cranks.
- Keep your elbows and knees loose, butt slightly off the saddle.
- Approach the lip at walking speed or faster.
- Don't hesitate at the lip.
- Look past the rim.
- Shift your weight rearward as the bike angles down.
- After the drop-in, adjust your weight if necessary.
- To slow, gently squeeze both brakes at the same time. Let up on the rear and increase pressure on the front if the rear wheel skids.
- If the front wheel skids, let up slightly on the brake; steer into the skid.
- As you hit level ground, return your body to a neutral position.
- Release the brakes to maintain momentum.

any downhill. Not enough to miss the fun, anyway.

Earthsurfing 101

Here's the downhiller's training drill: Once a week, ride to your practice hill and do five runs down it, going *slower* each time. That's right—slower. Do the first one at a walking pace; you should progress at a near standstill on the final run. Controlling your bike in super slo-mo, when balance is tougher than ever, embeds the skills into whatever part of your psyche stores skills. When you start going faster or steeper, the technique will still be there. Here's what to practice.

Set up for safe descending: Keep elbows and knees loose, pedals level, butt back, and use both brakes.

* **Set up your bike and body.** Shift to a gear that keeps your chain from slapping against your bike or shaking loose—usually a middle ring/largest cog combo, although some riders do big ring/middle cog so the chain covers the teeth of the big ring. (A big ring scar on your calf is a rite of passage, however.) Level your cranks at 3 and 9 o'clock so they don't anchor on the lip of the drop or on a rock or log. Stay loose in the ready position.

* **Approach at a walking pace.** To gain confidence and experience, you're controlling your descent. This won't happen if you're already past your comfort zone when you drop in. But don't approach so slowly that your front wheel stalls at the edge. And never hesitate at the lip—you'll fall hard just after you start down.

* **Look past the rim.** Focus on the part of the trail you want to ride to. If you stare at the rim, a steep section, a rut, or a pretty bunny, you will steer into it. (All except the bunny.)

* **Shift your weight back.** As the bike angles down, slide to the rear of the saddle—the steeper the hill, the more you move back. You shift your center of gravity to keep the bike from upending you.

WHO HAS THE RIGHT OF WAY?

When you're jamming downhill and see a group of riders inching their way toward you, who yields—the mountain biker who's having more fun or the ones working harder?

Downhillers always yield. That doesn't mean you need to stop. It means you slow down and, through eye contact or talking, find out which side you should pass on. Kind of a bummer, but you'll appreciate it when you're the miserable climber.

* **Adjust your weight.** Most novices move too far back. When this happens, the front wheel becomes "light" and skitters around. If that happens, just scoot forward slightly—don't hit the brake, which will be your first instinct.
* **Brakes, brakes, brakes.** Never slam the brakes—the ground will slam you. When descending, strive for smoothness in all things—the approach, the weight shift, the braking. Use both brakes at the same time, gently squeezing them until the bike is slowing but not skidding. You'll probably skid the rear wheel at first. This tears up the earth, which is bad and doesn't slow you any; it also lessens your control. If the rear skids, ease off and increase pressure on the front.

  Most braking power comes from the front—so much that you can flip yourself over the bar if you apply too much when your weight isn't rearward. If you make the weight shift, the front wheel will begin to skid before it tosses you over the bar. When it skids, ease off the lever until it begins rolling again, then gradually re-squeeze. If the skid continues, steer into it (shift your body weight instead of turning the handlebar).
* **Roll out.** As you reach bottom, return to a neutral position over the saddle. If you don't, you'll have too much weight to the rear and you won't be set up to handle the upcoming trail. Let go of the brakes. Be smooth and you can milk big momentum out of even teeny runouts.

Turn, Baby, Turn

When the singletrack slices sharp to the right, your mountain bike doesn't. It's a bad, bad feeling.

Inertia and your angle of approach—and perhaps your own silliness for trying to follow pro mountain biker Dave Wiens on a Colorado singletrack outside of his hometown of Gunnison—have combined to sling your bike along a fat arc that, at its apex, will flip you off the trail instead of guiding you to safety. You can see the scratchy, sandy surface where your body will make an imprint. You can see the stubby green bushes whose stickered arms will attempt to undress you as you roll by. And there, that rock—it's just the right size to crack your helmet.

Sometimes desperation is splendid. Without knowing exactly why, you point your right elbow and knee out. Maybe Dave did it, but you're not sure. There's an unsettling, shifting sensation beneath you, as if the bike picked itself up and hopped four inches to the right. (How did it do that?) Suddenly, you've abandoned your errant path and dived safely into the turn. You're through it. You're safe. Dave is off his bike and standing just in front of you, smiling. He seems proud of you, but more likely he's relieved. Even so, it doesn't matter. You did it. You followed a pro through a turn.

That was my first good corner. It felt like I was wrecking, and I didn't find the guts to repeat the process until a couple of rides later, but I'd done it. I knew what it felt like, and I knew I could do it.

You need to know this, too. If you're like most beginners, you fall behind on group rides every time you thread through an un-straight section, which is most of them, no? You waste a lot of energy working so hard to catch up so often, and because you're behind so much you feel like you really stink at riding—when the truth is you just can't turn. Or, if you ride by yourself, every turn slows you and sucks away the rush that comes with a speedy rhythm.

When you learn to turn you will be able to link all your other skills together into a flowing, fun ride that is faster and at the same time more secure than seemed possible. It's a good, good feeling.

Your Turn

The second-best place to practice carving is on a wide, level curve. The best place is on your lawn, with a fake curve marked by leaves or water bottles or those bright flowers from the garden. This way you can move the border to make the corner wider or tighter.

Go through your corner at slow speeds to practice the movements, then once you feel comfortable repeat the corner a little faster each time. Eventually the wheels will skitter and skip, but the techniques that got you through at 10 mph will zing you through at 20. When you wreck, you went too fast. That's easy to remember.

* **Plan your path to approach wide, cut inside across the turn, and exit wide.** This "flattens" the curve and minimizes the amount of lean you'll need. It also lets you ride a more direct line (you go almost straight through the curve instead of turning), which helps traction on loose surfaces. Sometimes the terrain won't let you go as wide as you want, but aim for the best line you can get.

* **Brake before the turn.** You should be at the speed you want before you begin the turn. If you carry too much speed into a corner you won't be able to hold your line. You'll either fly off the trail or try to brake, which washes out your wheels. Even if you recover, your rhythm and swoop are disrupted. It's safer and faster to brake before entering a curve. A novice who surfs an entire turn at a smooth 15 gets through quicker than one who enters at 17 and brakes to 13. (Experts brake extremely late in turns—but learn this method first.)

* **Stop pedaling.** If the terrain is rough, keep your cranks horizontal so you don't catch one on a rock or log. On smooth surfaces you can keep the outside pedal down to improve traction. Never put your inside pedal down—you *will* wreck and the other beginners will laugh at you.

lean into the turn and weight the outside pedal for traction

ride wide/inside/wide

Turns feel natural with the right path and good traction.

* **Lean into the turn.** Press down on the grip that's on the inside and angle the bike over. At slow speeds, or for tighter corners, you'll need to steer slightly inward, too. Don't worry about being tentative and not getting much lean. As you gain confidence in your traction, you'll slant more.
* **Stick your bike to the ground with body weight.** This gives you traction by driving the tire treads into the surface—counteracting the forces that want to push your bike out from under you. One method is to push down against the outside pedal. Some riders stay seated and transfer their weight straight down through the seat post. Others move the bike underneath them until it's on the inside track and their body's on the outside. Even the opposite—bike outside, body inside—can be effective. Play with all the variations to find the one that feels most natural for you.
* **Correct your line with elbow and knee swings.** If you ride too wide—which you will whenever the speed gets beyond your comfort level—ignore the instinct to crank the handlebar inward. This gets messy. Instead, pop your limbs out toward the inside corner. This pulls your bike into a tighter line, which is a swell feeling.
* **Accelerate out.** After you pass the apex, jam on the pedals. If you do it at just the right instant, you'll feel as if the turn is slinging you out onto the trail. If you don't get this feeling, you're waiting too long to begin pedaling. If you stick a pedal in the ground, or start

to get the sensation and then lose it, you're pedaling too soon.

A Turn for the Worse

Why did your turn suck? Here's what novices do wrong.

* **Not enough lean or weighting to maintain traction.** Beginners just won't believe that a bicycle will hold as well as it can on freaky surfaces. But it will. It's physics or something. Lean and press. Lean and press.
* **Not enough confidence.** A well-weighted, leaning, turning bike makes adjustments on its own. These movements probably feel like the beginning of wrecks to you—so you bail. Stay with the turn.
* **Too much speed.** If you feel like you're doing everything right but you still can't stick a turn, then stop trying. You're a novice. Go slow and enjoy the day. You'll be faster tomorrow. Wait until you're a great rider to rail every corner at eye-watering speeds.
* **Too much turn.** The techniques above are ideal for wide, level corners or banked curves. You'll need other moves for sharp turns, off-camber corners (which fall downhill on the outside), and much-littered, washboarded, or rutted turns. You'll get those moves.

Life in the Balance

You are on. It's one of those days when there's no difference between the trail and the bike, when you feel as if you're riding the earth itself, nothing between the two of you, no metal or rubber to mistranslate intention and act. It should always be like this, shouldn't it? Maybe this is the turning point—maybe from here it always will be like this. And as soon as you think that it ends, because you thought that.

Dumbass. Poser. I'd caught the edge of the wave I'd heard about so many times (only heard about), and instead of riding

do a good turn

- Enter the curve wide, cut inside, and exit wide.
- Brake before the turn.
- Stop pedaling and keep the cranks horizontal (or put the outside pedal down for more traction).
- Lean into the turn.
- Increase traction by pushing down on the outside pedal.
- If you go wide, pull into a tighter line by swinging your inside elbow and knee toward the inside corner.
- Sling out of the turn by jamming on the pedals after the apex but before the exit.

it out I started thinking about riding it out. I still make that same mistake, and I still call myself names when I do it. I think we all lose the flow way more often than we get lost in the flow. There's just no way to predict when you'll become mindless and perfect.

But you can learn to get yourself to the edge of that wave more often—and more chances means more successes. The key is balance.

Novices tend to think of balance in one dimension: If you lose it, you fall. That's true. But balance, like momentum, is one of those elements that affects everything we do on a mountain bike. Balance is someplace—usually someplace big—in every technique.

Watch the great riders. Their balance is so sharp that they use their bikes not like machines beneath them but like another limb; they move their bodies in relation to their bikes the way you can close your eyes and touch a finger to your nose.

You can become one of those honed riders—and you will if you simply ride long enough. You will learn the subtle balances that get you through turns quicker, keep the wheels on the ground for more stability (or lift them when necessary), shoot across lines until you find the best one, pause momentarily during slow-speed sections to plan your choreography, climb better, and do lots of other advanced techniques. Just ride a long time.

Or you can practice. You can focus on the cool stuff balance can do for you rather than learning just enough to avoid its detriments (which is what most beginners do). This involves some useful things, like learning to balance your bike at a standstill, as well as some crazy acts, like riding with your eyes closed. But if you take the time now (while your beginner brain is still impressionable) to understand how your weight placement affects the bike, you'll save yourself a lot of name-calling.

Balancing Acts

Do this stuff and you can finally tell your mother that you're well balanced. She'll be so proud of you.

✸ **Do a trackstand.** Balancing your bike at a standstill is easier than it appears. After four or five practice sessions you should nail a 20- or 30-second balancing act. The reason it seems so difficult is that few riders really practice. Most people work on this only during down time—before or after a ride—with only three or four attempts before quitting. Dedicate a half hour every other day to this skill and you'll become a thoroughly honed gnarly person. Ride to a slight incline. Level your cranks to the horizontal position, then turn your front wheel slightly toward the side your forward pedal is on. Apply enough pedal pressure to keep from rolling backward, but not so much that you roll forward. (If you do, straighten the front wheel slightly and let yourself roll back.) You can use the front brake for more control if you want.

Sometimes not moving at all is the best move of all. Apply brakes for more control; turn the wheel in the same direction as the forward pedal; and apply light pedal pressure.

* **Fall off narrow things.** That is, try to ride narrow things (but you learn more from falling). A 2 **x** 4 laid flat is good. My favorites are curbs and parking blocks. To keep your bike rolling on such surfaces you need to do all of your "steering" with your body instead of with the handlebar. Trying to do this forces you into all kinds of little tricks—counterbalances and opposing-weight stuff—that are impossible to explain but that will develop naturally with practice.

* **Dance with your bike.** Go to a field or a parking lot. At slow speed, swing your body all over the place and see how much you can make the bike match—or oppose—your movements. Can you make your bike tip left when your chest goes right? Can you lift the rear wheel even if your weight is centered over it? The goal is to get your body and bike into awkward juxtapositions and then find out how to bring both back under control. You'll appreciate this skill someday when you get all twisted up at high speed and can pull out of it.

* **Ride with your eyes shut.** (But not on a trail. Please.) Pedal across a wide, long, unpopulated, grassy field, then close your eyes for three strokes. Work up to 10 or more if you have the guts and the room. The sensation is freaky, and riding blind is not a skill you'll ever use unless things get really, really bad out on the trail one day. But without your vision you pay more attention to how the bike moves over terrain; each sideways sway or forward dip becomes magnified. It sounds stupid, but you're as close as you'll ever be able to get to feeling what the bike feels.

Fuel for Thought

Food is fuel. If you think of it that way, there's not much difference between, say, a tasty chocolate peanut butter energy snack or the green ant you just popped into your mouth.

That's what I told myself anyway when my Australian guide, Dan Foley, started picking the little critters off a strangling fig. "They taste lemony," he effused as he pinched a fingerful into his mouth. "But you better get their heads off quick or they sting. Ouch." He smiled.

Four hours into a day of rain forest singletrack—weaving through dense thickets of stinging bushes and barbed thorns, pedaling through hub-deep tributaries that probably (but not definitely) weren't infested with crocs, falling down the sides of mountains and calling it biking—we needed fuel, not necessarily food.

We'd already tried harvesting some kind of chewy, star-shaped fruit that after a few bites stopped tasting like itself and took on the flavor of my own mouth. Next was something that looked like an orange but was so bitter it seized my throat, making it impossible to swallow or spit back up. ("Usually a bit sweeter," Dan said.) In a few hours we'd fall out of the rain forest and flail our way to a backroad garage where Dan would spring for meat pies—an Aussie blue-collar delicacy

How to Balance Your Bike at a Standstill

Here are six steps to learning the technique bike geeks call a trackstand. Some people use the front brake for more control, but a brakeless stand is purer. When you get good on an incline, move to level ground.

* Ride to a slight incline; slow to a stop.
* Level your cranks.
* Turn your front wheel slightly in the direction of the forward pedal.
* Apply just enough pedal pressure to keep from rolling backward—not enough to roll forward.
* If you begin moving forward, straighten the front wheel slightly and let yourself roll back.
* Maintain an equilibrium between forward and backward forces.

akin to the good old gas station weenie.

I think of it, fondly now, as the Day of Disturbing Food. But it kept me riding.

Clutch Carbo

Sometimes fuel is all you need. You just want to keep riding. But most of the time —especially when you're a new rider or a casual, recreational gnarly person—nutrition should be a party instead of a duty.

Pro racers are hardened machines who sometimes must ingest up to 10,000 calories per day (about five times the average) because they need to do their jobs—an approach that drains the fun out of one of life's greatest pleasures. If you begin racing seriously or reach the level where you begin testing yourself on long, grueling epics, you'll have to learn to hydrate and feed yourself by the numbers. Until then, your goal is simple: Keep the party going but take in enough energy and fluid to also keep yourself riding strong.

What most beginners think of as a lack of fitness is really lack of energy. Leg cramps, failing arms, fading concentration—you succumb to all of these frailties (and others) when your tank goes empty. If you keep yourself fed and watered you can ride farther than you ever thought possible.

Rules for cycling nutrition really aren't much different than for other sports (or for plain old life, for that matter). *Carbohydrate* is the chief source of fuel for your body because it's easily transformed into glucose and glycogen, sugars that can be quickly used by muscles. You also use *fat* for energy, but it's a less-efficient fuel. *Protein* can be used for energy when your other supplies are severely depleted, but your body mainly uses it to rebuild muscles. So your diet should be mostly carbo—somewhere between 60 and 70 percent. About 20 to 30 percent of your total calories should come from fat, 10 to 15 percent from protein.

That's it. Everything else is just a mat-

If it makes your body go, it's good for you.

ter of knowing how and when to get that mix into your body. Here's how to keep riding strong and steady.

* **You don't need food unless you're riding more than 90 minutes**. The sugar in your blood and muscles can fuel most efforts shorter than that.

* **Eat before you're hungry.** If you know you'll be riding long, begin nibbling about 30 to 45 minutes into the epic. Food takes some time to get into your system, especially when your body is concentrating on pedaling instead of digesting. If you don't eat until you're empty, you'll never catch up. This is called a bonk, and it ain't pretty. You see spots. You see flying chili dogs. Backpackers beat you up hills.

* **Eat just enough.** Gluttony isn't only a sin and a sign of poor social skills, it's also a sure way to divert blood from your hard-working muscles to your bloated digestive system. How much is just enough? For most people it's about 20 grams of carbo for every 20 minutes of riding—about two bananas an hour, one pack of energy gel, or most of an

energy bar. A better guideline: Never be hungry, never be full.

* **Eat what tastes good.** Almost all the commercial energy snacks sold in bike shops meet or exceed the guidelines for good nutrition. (Look at the label if you're not sure.) Some of them are also stuffed with extra nutrients to help rebuild tissue, aid in energy conversion, and to help your body absorb and balance its fluid level. Other snacks avoid hi-sci mixes and go for natural combos that deliver the key ingredients. The important thing is to buy whatever tastes best to you, or whichever marketing hype presses your button. All cycling snacks work at this basic nutrition level, but none work if you don't eat them. Appeal is everything.

* **Go natural.** Gels and goos and bars and formulas are brought to us by the same brains that put humans on the moon and libraries on microchips. That's comforting. But sometimes nothing beats a banana (no fat, lots of carbo, and potassium, which helps balance your fluid level), a bagel (a carbo explosion with no fat), or a green ant (a protein delight). Especially in price.

* **Shove food through your glycogen window.** Immediately after a ride, your body is primed to replace the energy it's used—but the longer you wait, the less it stores in your muscles. The less you store, the worse you ride next time. Within an hour after a ride—before the window slams shut—eat about half a gram of carbo for every pound you weigh. For a 150-pound rider, that's about one banana and half a bagel. You don't need much, but it's key.

Going with the Flow

Along with your splendid food mix, you need enough liquid to keep your body hydrated—kind of like keeping your chain lubed or your car pistons oiled. If you don't, things seize up. Even becoming just a little low can be harmful—as little as a 2-percent drop in your fluid level can affect performance and make you ride like a boob. Thankfully, the basic rules for drinking are even simpler than those for eating.

* **Drink before you're thirsty.** That old never-catch-up rule again. I take a sip at least every 15 minutes and at the top of most hills (or on the way up if I need to pass time and the grade isn't too steep).

* **Drink just enough.** Your body needs at least four cups of water during every hour of moderate cycling to stay hydrated. That's about one bottle every 60 minutes. Unlike with food, not many novices drink too much water. If you do it's usually not a huge problem—you just have to pee more than everyone else.

* **Watch your urine color.** If your urine is yellow, you're not drinking enough. If you're not peeing, you're really not drinking enough.

* **Get plenty of carbo.** If you're using a carbo-mix drink, get one with at least 14 grams of carbohydrate per serving (about half a bottle). This way you won't have to flood yourself to get enough fuel. Energy drinks are a good way to rehydrate and refuel at the same time. But they're sticky. And if they're all you have, the formula will sometimes seem too thick and rich after a couple hours of riding. Take along some plain water, too.

* **Cut your juice, or spike your water.** Fill a bottle half with orange juice, half with water. It's quickly absorbed carbo for pennies a serving.

* **Wipe your bottle.** Riding covers your bottle with mud, stream water, dust, plant spores, and all kinds of little living things that can't wait to dance around inside your digestive system. Better safe than deathly ill.

Shred Lightly

Not everyone loves mountain biking as much as you do. In fact, some people hate it. And they'll hate you for doing it.

Some hikers, equestrians, naturalists, and other assorted cranks who try to close trails to mountain bikes believe that we trash the earth and shred the serenity of nature. Lots of studies have shown that mountain bikes have negligible impact on properly designed trails (way less than horse hooves, for sure), but—as much I hate to admit it—I think the second half of their contention is true more often than it should be.

I've witnessed boneheads buzzing hikers, scaring horses into panic gallops, staging unofficial races on busy trails, rampaging through sections obviously set up for slow riding, and committing other acts of stupidity. Those are the people I hate. They're ruining our sport—and getting our trails closed. I hope no one reading this book becomes one of those riders, but these days it seems many beginners do. There's a harder edge to our sport, which is cool, but we can shred lightly, as Ibis guru Scot Nicol likes to say.

The International Mountain Bicycling Association, an organization that works for trail access and promotes responsible riding, created six Rules of the Trail to help us do just that.

* **Ride on open trails only.** Some routes are closed during access disputes; others are too sensitive for fat tires. Ride either type and you're damaging something.
* **Leave no trace.** Skids are cool only on race courses, where a crew repairs all that damage. Ride rainy trails only if the storm starts after the ride. And don't rearrange the trail for your convenience—learn to ride the mountain instead of making the mountain rideable.
* **Control your bicycle.**

* **Always yield the trail.** Some riders dismount to let hikers and horses pass. I'm not that polite, but I always slow for hikers and horse riders, steer to the edge of the trail, make eye contact, and say something friendly. Ask equestrians the best way to approach their horses.
* **Never spook animals.** Most of us—including me—give in to the occasional bunny chase. But I never ride off the trail after the cuddly little things. Try not to be an Ugly Human on a consistent basis.
* **Plan ahead.** Don't get lost, stranded without a spare tube, or caught without adequate dental coverage.

eat . . .
- Eat only on rides longer than 90 minutes.
- Eat before you're hungry.
- Eat just enough.
- Carry tasty snacks.
- Remember the cheap natural stuff: bananas, bagels, and fig bars.
- Refuel as soon as possible after a ride.

. . . drink . . .
- Drink before you're thirsty.
- Drink just enough.
- Yellow urine = not enough fluid intake.
- Choose a carbo-mix drink with at least 14 grams of carbo per serving. Also carry a bottle of plain water.
- Mix half orange juice/half water.

. . . and be wary . . .
- Wipe your bottle before drinking.

Always yield to Mr. Ed.
He's out of work.

Go Your Own Way

As novices, most of us spend most of our time following people—that's one of the ways we're supposed to learn how to ride. It works. Shift when they shift. Get out of the saddle when they do. Squeal your brakes when you hear theirs. Walk when they walk.

You don't understand why you're doing those things, but you do them, and pretty soon you associate the scenario with the action—and boom, you know a technique.

The problem is that you can become the mountain biking world's greatest follower. It happened to me. I felt so confident behind better riders—and so kludgy on my own—that I once didn't go on a solo ride for two months.

I was an idiot, riding with borrowed skills. Not only that, but I missed all those things the world rewards you with when you're alone on a bike: the scratch of leaves on their branches, water shushing across rocks, new trails that go nowhere, fixing a flat under a tree on a sunny day and deciding to take a nap, hearing your heart follow its own beat instead of someone else's.

You'll never be more than a novice until you prove to yourself that your skills are real. And you'll never be able to let your bike speak if you spend all your time listening to other people. Your bike has interesting things to say. It hears things you can't—things the trail tells it. You will not believe this until it happens. Go take a ride.

By yourself.

Besides all the spiritual crap—and I do think speaking with your bike is both authentically spiritual and, in some sense, crap—riding alone has a practical purpose. You will be able to absorb the skills that other people have laid on you. When your pace and direction are your own you can practice (and re-practice) and experiment (and re-experiment) and even fail (and re-fail). No one will laugh or get impatient except you. Here are some things to try by yourself.

* **Ride alternate lines.** The group's good line might not be yours. When I started riding alone I realized that I'm good at uphill wheelies. So when the group veers away from uphill jumps I crank straight up and over. Ride familiar paths in new ways and you'll discover new strengths—and perhaps weaknesses, which is just as good a lesson.
* **Practice the impossible.** When I'm trying to stay with the train, my goal is not necessarily to ride everything, but to get over everything at the group's pace—walk, run, swim, or fall. When I solo, I stop and try tough stuff again. And again. (But never more than three times, which is my own magic frustration barrier.)
* **Do stupid things.** Ride hills in your big ring. Use too much front brake. Why? So you know what mistakes feel like and how to recover from them. You might also surprise yourself. By riding overgeared I discovered that on rollers I like to stand and hammer in the middle ring instead of scooting along in the small one like my mentors always did.
* **Cream the easy stuff.** Sections that were once challenges to me are now mere throughways—my friends and I scorch through them to get to the new, fun stuff. But sometimes I go back alone to the simple trails and relish how much better I am. I tell myself I'm the man. I feel cool. Just don't get caught looking self-congratulatory on a wimpy trail.

SHRED U: HIGHER STUDIES IN GETTING HONED

YOU push your bike off and settle onto the saddle before you clip both feet in, flowing along the twisty, brambled opening of the trail you love so much. There's that little hill, only as high as your waist but steeper than anything else on the ride, and you bob over it like a bird on a calm wave, then slow so you can trickle your bike through the rocks dotting the next section.

You love your trail, and that's all you're thinking about, except you aren't even thinking: You're *feeling*. You realize you're pedaling but you don't remember clicking in. You haven't thought about a single technique the whole time you've been on your bike.

You're not a beginner anymore. You probably haven't been for a while. That's the way it works. There's no graduation ceremony or pay increase. You can't even identify the ride when things changed. Before this one there was the time you cleaned that rock field, and that other ride when you finally made the long climb up that loose scut, and that last sunny Saturday of the year when you romped over your friends.

You still ride like a beginner sometimes. You still get the wobbles; you miss turns and drift off the trail and mis-time wheelies so badly your front tire smacks logs and rebounds the stem into your stomach. But you're not a beginner.

You still rely on the same basic skills that you force-fed into your uncooperative body when you knew nothing. You'll use that foundation as long as you ride a mountain bike. But now there's a difference. You're not using those techniques just to survive. They've set you free.

Most of this chapter will help you refine those basic skills and add new techniques to your repertoire—and as an intermediate you're going to ride faster, longer, higher, and safer (usually—some of us just keep wrecking more and more). But those aren't the things that release you from beginnerhood. Neither is the ability to use techniques without concentrating on them or conquering unconquerable obstacles (or riders)—though those are the things you'll probably notice.

The difference is a pair of intangibles woven throughout your riding: You mountain bike with *anticipation* and the ability to *link*.

An . . . ticipation

When you began riding you learned to use your vision to steer your bike—to look where you wanted to go instead of where you didn't. You also trained yourself to look farther ahead instead of directly in front of your wheels to avoid surprises.

But anticipation is about more than

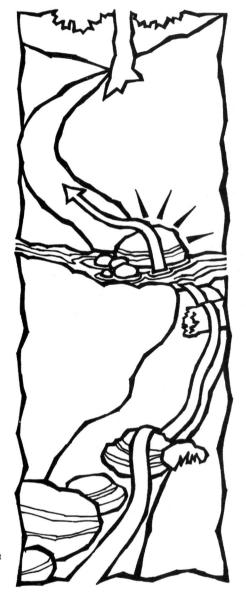

Plan your line so you're set up to clean a section's hardest challenge.

avoiding surprises. It's about finding the ultimate good line—not just the best line to solve the problem you're facing this second, or even in the next 10 or 60 seconds. Riders who anticipate pick out a section's peak move—the area that will require the most skill or power (or both) to clear. Or the area where the greatest gain can be made in a race. Or where the most fun can be had. Whatever the system of measurement, the section tops out.

The whole trail becomes a choreographed dance leading to the peak move. Instead of riding the best line move by move, you ride to give yourself the best peak line. You don't think *rock . . . rock . . . dip . . . avoidable log . . . shallow part of creek . . . uphill lunge.* You think *rock . . . rock . . . dip and come out really spinning so I can take the log to set up straighter for the deep part of the creek so my wheel bites that big rock with better traction instead of the little ones right before the peak uphill lunge.*

You're already beginning to do this. If you concentrate on picking out peak moves you'll develop your anticipation even faster.

Not Missing Links

You've also begun to link basic moves into something that resembles what rock climbers call a dynamic technique—like when they spring upward and grab for a new handhold simultaneously.

The most common dynamic technique I see fresh intermediates make is a wheelie turn—lifting the front wheel and shifting it to one side at the same time. Sound familiar? You can also combine braking and weight shifts to move your bike sideways or slow it quicker.

There are lots of dynamic moves—the combinations might not be endless but they're close enough to it that I'd rather spend my time riding than counting them. And they're almost as difficult to dissect as

to catalog, so don't look for any descriptions here.

What's important is that you open yourself to the improvisation that leads to dynamic moves. Stop concentrating on one technique at a time—sometimes stop concentrating on technique altogether and just tell your body to get your bike through a section and see what happens. You've become good enough for that.

Rise and Shine

The top of the hill flicks from side to side, bobbing to the extreme borders of your vision as you sway over the bike. You can feel the wheels biting into the hard bone of the incline now, every stroke of the pedals like the draw of a dull saw instead of a whirring spin, and your lungs begin to become solid, heavy things that press against your chest.

Here is where you pray to the crest, "Once more, please. Please. Let me top out again. Let me make this one again, like the good riders." But today there is no prayer. You think about how your lungs always ache this bad, and how those black spots always flutter just in front of you but never stop you like they used to, and without planning it you click up a gear and rise out of the saddle and attack the hill.

You've just graduated to intermediate climber. It happened to me a year after I began riding—on the longest, steepest, rockiest local climb. For the first time my goal wasn't just to get to the top but to get there with some speed, to get there ahead of a few other riders I'd always considered better, to get there with some style.

That climb changed my perspective. Since then, even when I'm on a fresh (and sometimes unrideable) incline, I climb with a strategy of producing more sustained power while using less energy. That ideal came to me complete and unbidden, but the tips to make it work took years more of riding.

You won't make every crest with these tips. No one does. Not even the best. But when you stop climbing just to survive you will climb faster, longer, and be able to go steeper than you did before. On the climbs you always made as a novice you'll conserve more energy for the plunge down the other side (or for mounting the next hill).

When climbing, pick a line that avoids technical sections.

The three basics you learned as a beginner—ride in the climber's position, learn to maintain traction, understand when to stand—are still necessities. These tips are glorious luxuries.

Going Long

What's a long climb? That depends on you and the terrain. Sometimes it's five minutes. Sometimes it's 105. Instead of judging by time, think of a long climb as one that you could ride better by using one—or all—of these tips.

Short stuff requires only a simple strategy: sit and pedal, stand if you need to, then sit again if you need to, and you're up (or off). When you go long, you need more.

* **Don't leak momentum.** Every time you hit an obstacle you lose a little momentum. If the climb is short and you are fresh you easily regain your pace. But hit 25 or 50 momentum thieves and you've done a lot of extra work. Take the best, shortest line you can find (which means don't ride 50 feet out of your way to avoid a twig).

* **Plan ahead on technical climbs.** When a sloppy line surprises you on downhills or flats, it's usually just a temporary inconvenience. You can flail over the obstacle and get back on the good line. But a long, technical climb drains your energy so that you might not have the oomph to power over unexpected obstacles. Plan your lines farther ahead. For instance, you might want to take a steeper line to the right to set yourself up to miss those slippery roots on the left 20 feet away.

* **Pace off other people.** While we all tend to settle into our own pace on a long climb, you can sometimes elevate your effort by concentrating on other riders. If someone comes around you, try to hang on to the rear wheel. If someone fades in from the horizon,

you're gaining. Chase. (Most of us ride harder when we're trying to catch people than when we're trying to stay in front of them.) But be careful—don't ride so hard you blow. If you can't hold someone's pace, back off to your speed.

✱ **Pace your breathing.** The strain of climbing can cause us to hold our breath or take short, uneven pants. This is bad. Synchronize your breath to pedal strokes; search for a rhythm that gives you long, measured breaths. You can also prevent panting by exhaling forcefully instead of putting the effort into inhaling. This takes some practice—hard inhale/passive exhale is the natural pattern.

✱ **Alternate muscles.** Slide toward the rear of your saddle to use more of your butt muscles. You'll have greater pedaling power (but less efficient use of energy) than when you're forward on the saddle using more of your leg muscles. Give both sets a workout. You can also

Climbing in the saddle uses your strong butt muscles and is more efficient than standing.

vary your muscle use with your chest position. Sit with your upper body bent about 45 degrees and you use mostly butt muscles; sit more upright and you

Fool yourself into climbing stronger with a mental bungee cord. It works.

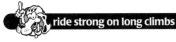
ride strong on long climbs

- Avoid obstacles.
- Plan ahead.
- Pace off a passing rider; chase those in front.
- Synchronize your breathing to pedal strokes; exhale forcefully.
- Vary muscle use.
- Use an imaginary bungee cord.
- Don't be demoralized by false flats; don't waste energy by attacking false summits.

draw on the thighs.

★ **Bungee.** This sounds stupid, but it works. Pick an object 10 to 30 yards up the climb—a tree or large rock. Toss a mental bungee cord around the object and let the cord pull you up. Apparently, our ignorant bodies can be fooled by our clever brains.

★ **Don't get faked out.** False flats—sections that rise so gradually the incline isn't obvious—make you feel like a loser because you think you're too wasted to cruise on level ground. Look behind you—it's easier to see a false flat going down than up. False summits are even more demoralizing: The climb appears to crest so you surge—and see another crest half a mile up. To avoid being fooled, look off the trail. If you see trees or more mountain above the "peak," you're not near the peak.

Going Steep

Just as there is no absolute definition of long, steep is in the misery of the beholder. I define steep as anything I can't walk down, anything I'd drop off the back of the saddle to ride down, anything I need to row up.

Rowing up a hill is a cool technique I learned from John Olsen, one of those gods in my all-time-hall-of-coolness pantheon. In about 15 minutes he taught me how to ascend a trail I'd been attempting for two years. Rowing is a skill to use when a climb is so severe that no matter how much you shift your weight back and forth you can't find a position that keeps your front wheel on the ground and your rear full of traction.

Here's the move: Scoot forward until the nose of the saddle pokes

Nothing's too steep to climb! Scoot forward until the saddle pokes between your butt cheeks and pull the bar down and back with every pedal stroke.

between your butt cheeks. (You're not sitting on the saddle; you're floating almost in front of it.) Lean over the handlebar—the steeper the slope the more you lean. With each pedal stroke pull back and down on the handlebar, almost as if you're holding oars and rowing yourself up the hill. You won't get the timing right at first, but when it clicks you'll never do it wrong again.

Your weight keeps the front wheel down and the force you apply to the handlebar digs the back wheel down. The pedal strokes feel hard even in the easiest gear combo, and pulling the handlebar will tire your upper body quickly, but as long as your muscles hold out you can climb things that look impossible to your friends (and to you once you're up and have to get back down).

Radical Descents

You can't even ride to the beginning of the Wattle-Blower trail in Queensland, Australia. You have to hike there. And then, catching your breath, you stand on a bare hummock atop a mountain that makes the forest below look like a manicured lawn. A dusty groove slices down and away from you into a section of rock—the mountain's open wound. Plunge through that, thread through those trees, don't drift too far to the left after the rocks (that's the edge of the mountain there), and then the ride really begins.

Standing before some-

thing like that your throat closes, and when you swallow against the pressure you get a taste as if you've been licking your bike frame: metallic fear. Or joy. Whichever—it ain't ordinary life.

Down and Dirty

Just going fast enough can make any descent radical. It's mountain biking's reciprocating rush theory: The tamer the terrain, the higher the speed required. To rad out with speed downhill, you use the same

conquer the steepest climbs

- **Weight the front wheel.**
- **With each pedal stroke, pull backward and down on the handlebar to drive the rear wheel into the ground.**

Don't fight a descent—go with it and focus on control. Remember: The steeper the pitch, the more you move back. Steer with your hips instead of the handlebar and modulate brakes to prevent skids.

riding steep downhills

- Set up in descending position.
- Shift your weight way back.
- Steer with your hips.
- Feather the brakes.
- Avoid skidding if possible; when a skid is unavoidable, steer into it.
- Be prepared for a freaky roll out.

skills you use for going faster on the flats—handling quick turns, extending your vision, soaking up bumps, and other techniques.

But the brand of gnarliness we're talking about here comes strictly from steepness. Severe pitches magnify the difficulty of everything. The techniques needed for riding your personal Wattle-Blowers are similar to the basic skills you already learned. Like the angle of descent, you just exaggerate everything.

WEAVING VS. SKIDDING

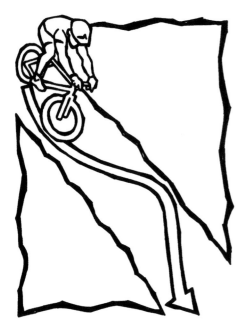

In grooves or loose scut, weave to avoid out-of-control skidding.

Instead of accepting a skid and trying to maintain control by steering into it, some riders regain control by weaving across the trail. This works especially well when the trail is grooved and filled with loose material. Your side-to-side line scrubs off speed like a third brake. Weaving can be bad if the line is too wide—it will widen the trail, which is an eco no-no. But even then it's usually less damaging than skidding.

* **Set up in the descending position.** Level cranks, loose elbows and knees, butt grazing the saddle instead of resting on it. Your chain should be on the big ring to cover the teeth in case you wreck.

* **Shift your weight back as you drop in.** On a rad descent, go way back. (I've had my butt off the back of the saddle and hanging just inches above the rear tire.) In this position it's impossible to endo; all you have to worry about is side-to-side balance. You almost never need that extreme weight shift, but you'll still be farther back than normal. Practice this on flat ground before you try it on a descent. You have to understand how to extend your arms and legs but keep them flexy. You don't want to try to learn that when your bike is diving.

* **Steer by moving your hips, not the handlebar.** With so much of your weight back, the front wheel is light. Don't give it a chance to skitter. Keep it straight.

* **Feather the brakes.** On long descents your hands will tire from continually depressing the brake levers. Good riders avoid this by modulating the lever in and out so rapidly that braking force isn't affected, but over the course of the descent your hands are given a zillion short rest breaks that add up to one decent one.

* **Avoid skids if possible.** Not going to happen on the steepest stuff. Keep the skid minimal by using as much front brake as possible. But when you get into a long one, steer your bike (with your hips) in the direction of the skid to regain control.

* **Be prepared for freaky handling in the roll out.** You have so much weight in the back that re-entry is guaranteed to be weird. If you move forward too soon or too quickly you catch more of

the shock from the compression as the bike levels out. Any roll out is rideable, but the sensation is unsettling.

Lunge Time

The boulder is hub high, and it waits for you in the same spot it always does, with the same expression it always has—the expression that says, "You're mine."

And it's right. You are. You've never cleaned that boulder.

Part of the problem is fatigue—by the time you grunt up half the hill to where the boulder sits you're too blown for a good, rock-scaling power stroke. Part of the problem is confidence—you *know* you can't clean the thing. But most of the problem is ignorance—aside from going fast and hoping for the best, you just don't know how to ride something that big on an uphill.

My usual routine for conquering big stuff (popping the front wheel over, then shifting my weight into a neutral position and pedaling over) rewarded me with nothing but multicolored calves. Pretty, but not really worth the pain. So I'd given up on the boulder.

Then one day I was so tired that I got my front wheel on top of the thing before I'd thought about what I was doing. (Extreme fatigue can be a real asset—it shuts your brain up and shakes instinct awake.) I teetered on the rock, moved my body weight forward, and shoved the bike away from me.

I cleaned the damned thing. I'd found the lunge.

The All-Purpose Move

The lunge is a technique not only for getting over medium-size uphill obstacles (about hub high) but really big stuff (taller than your wheel) on the flats. You can use it to cross rocks and logs, get out of gulches and gullies, scale steep banks, and quickly flee theaters showing movies in which Meryl Streep uses a foreign accent. Once

Lunge across obstacles you can't hop by pushing the bike up and over. This is really cool.

how to lunge

- **Approach at walking pace.**
- **Loft the front of your bike and set the front wheel on the obstacle.**
- **Bend your knees; move your head and chest forward over the handlebar.**
- **Keep the cranks horizontal.**
- **Do a pedaling lunge: Let the chainrings roll into the obstacle, then stroke the pedal as you push the handlebar away from you.**
- **Do a hopping lunge: Before the chainrings roll into the obstacle, spring upward as you push the handlebar away from you.**
- **Get down by pushing the handlebar forward and down.**
- **Shift your weight back so the front wheel doesn't stick in the ground, then shift forward so the rear wheel lands lightly.**

you understand the lunge, you'll find all kinds of other uses for it. You will love the lunge, and it will love you. Here's how to start this glorious relationship.

* Approach the obstacle at walking pace.
* Compress the wheel with a weight shift, then lift (pull sharply back and up on the bar as you give a hard pedal stroke) when you're about one wheel length from the obstacle. You want to set your front wheel on top of the object.
* As the front wheel contacts the top, position your body to deliver the lunge: Bend your knees, move your head and chest forward until they're over the handlebar. The funny physics of doing this—moving your body over a moving bike—creates a counterforce that slows the bike. Don't freak out. Be sure the cranks are horizontal—if one is hanging down, it'll catch on the obstacle when you lunge. Your face will become dirty. Or worse.
* Now comes the lunge: You're going to shove your bike forward (away from you), pushing it up onto the log while your body stays behind. This will seem impossible when you're balanced at a crazy angle on a big scary hard thing. But even the weakest mountain bikers are strong enough to push their bikes, right? (Don't you roll it along beside you all the time?) You just didn't know you could do it while you're sitting over it.

You can choose between a pedaling lunge or a hopping lunge. Both work. To pedal atop a log, let the bike roll forward until the chainring bites into the obstacle. Then stroke the pedal to grind up on the log, simultaneously pushing the handlebar away from you. To do a hopping lunge, spring upward before the chainring rolls into the obstacle (pull the rear up with your feet) as you push the handlebar away from you.

* It doesn't matter if you do the grind or the hop: Your body is now centered over the chainrings, which are perched atop the obstacle; your rear wheel is touching the back of the object; your front hangs free. You have become a teeter-totter. Get down by unbalancing yourself—push the handlebar forward and down.
* Shift some weight back to keep the front wheel from sticking the ground when it lands. As the rear comes off, shift some weight forward to soften its impact.

Air Apparent

Bunnyhops. Jumps. Life. Until it happens to you, you don't believe that sometimes there's an instant at the top of an airborne arc when the world stops moving while you fly over the globe—following the curve of our funky sphere—and everything is silent and your bike just seems to pause and hang there.

And then the world starts moving again, faster than you've ever seen it—right up at you, fast, fast, fast. And the rush of air across your ears stuns you. You can hear your tires spinning on nothing and wham! Whoo! Wow! Gotta try that again.

Airing out is life. It is freedom from gravity and an acute consciousness of it all at once. It is the smoothest path over obstacles with the potential to become the roughest. It is quick, but can stretch out seconds like few other experiences in mountain biking. And it is, most of all, *so* cool.

The ability to "get air" has always been a dividing line between the competent and the honed, and it always will be. It's not a necessary technique. There are other ways over any obstacle, and those ways are usually safer (and sometimes just as quick). Watch a pro cross-country race and you'll see the best riders in the world get off and shoulder their bikes over bad patches.

So why air? Because when you've milked a downhill for speed, slowing for a six-inch log feels like defeat. Because sometimes the rhythm of a ride demands it. Because people dig it. Because your friend did it. Because after you pop one, you want more.

There are two basic kinds of flying. The *bunnyhop* is when, from a more-or-less level surface, you leap over an obstacle. You usually go about 2 feet high and hop 4 to 8 feet. A *jump* is when you launch off some kind of ramp—either a man-made rise or a natural upslope. Good jumpers can travel more than 30 feet at an altitude in the double digits. Most of us jump 5 to 15 feet, never going higher than 5 feet or so. Here's how to dial in both kinds of air.

Hip Hops

A bunnyhop is less of a hop upward than it is a leap forward. You pull your bike up with your arms and feet, then push it forward in an arc over whatever obstacle you're trying to avoid. So don't think *up*, think *up and over*. Keep that in mind, and follow this sequence.

Wheels plus riding skill equals wings! Air out your local trail. After compressing the bike, pull up with hands and feet to start jump and rotate bar forward to lift your rear wheel.

* Approach faster than walking speed. Look at the obstacle until you're four to five feet away from it, then look past it to where you want to land.
* Push your body down into your bike by compressing your elbows and knees—you're preloading the bike to help it spring upward.
* Time the next move to begin when you're about one to two feet from the obstacle. You want to be close enough so your rear wheel doesn't smash into the object when you land, but far enough away so that the rear wheel doesn't knock against it on the way up, either. Only experience can teach you the perfect takeoff point.
* Pull up on the handlebar at the same time you sharply shift your weight up and back. Your arms and legs will straighten, and the front end will rise. How high it rises depends on how fast you make this transition and how fast your bike is moving. It's that experience thing again.
* Rotate your wrists forward like you're trying to twist the handlebar away from you. Combined with a slight push forward on the bar, this helps bring the rear wheel up.
* If you got the guts, you can gain more loft by pulling the bike up more with your hips, knees, and feet. It doesn't seem like you could do this when you're already airborne, but you can.
* If both wheels will touch ground at the same time, enjoy the remainder of your flight. If the rear wheel is riding slightly lower, you still can relax. But if the front is positioned to land first, pull up on the

handlebar—unless you're an expert or lucky, you'll wreck if the front wheel touches down before the back one does.
* As the bike lands, absorb the impact of the touchdown by bending your elbows and knees. On big hits, the handlebar can come all the way up to your chest.

Might As Well Jump

Unlike bunnyhops, jumps happen almost by accident. Carry enough speed onto any kind of ramp and you'll sail off it. You can grab more air—and giddiness—by doing what pros call *working the transition*. That means putting oomph into your takeoff. Here's how.

* Just like with a bunnyhop, compress into the bike to preload it, then spring upward. Time this to occur just as your front wheel leaves the ramp.
* You can control the height of the jump. To gain altitude, do the same in-flight second spring you do when bunnyhopping. If you want to stay lower—which is actually quicker (and safer when you're learning)—push your body down into the bike just after takeoff. Stay relaxed, though—don't try to keep the bike down with stiff elbows. Relax, let it come up, then push it down and forward. If you stiffen up at this point, your flight path will get really funky.
* Unlike bunnyhops, most jumps don't happen on level surfaces. You're usually doing downhill. On a gradual descent, aim to have both wheels hit ground at the same time. On a steep downhill, gently touch the front wheel first—but not with so much force or weight that you launch into a dangerous nose wheelie. Keep your weight back off the wheel.

One Good Turn

You are dancing, leading the trail and being led sometimes, sometimes letting it

how to bunnyhop

- **Approach faster than walking speed.**
- **Preload the bike.**
- **Initiate liftoff by pulling up on the handlebar and shifting your weight up and back. Time it so both wheels clear the obstacle.**
- **Bring the rear wheel up by pushing the handlebar forward and rotating your wrists toward the front of the bike.**
- **To go higher, pull up again with your hips, knees, and feet.**
- **If necessary, pull up on the handlebar so you land on the rear first, or (only if needed) on both wheels at once.**
- **Let the bike come up into you as you land.**

Jump farther by keeping your bike low—push your body down into it after you're airborne.

how to jump

- Compress the bike to preload it, then spring upward just as the front wheel leaves the ramp.
- Go higher by pulling up with your hips, knees, and feet; stay low by pushing your body down into the bike after takeoff.
- On level ground or gentle descents, land the rear wheel first or both wheels at once. On steep downhills, let the front wheel lightly touch first.

spin you back around to face the sunset, sometimes seeming to twirl the earth in whatever direction you choose. You have that touch tonight, that lightest of connections with the trail that also is the most secure, and it shows mostly in the turns. Swoops. Sweeps. Arcs. Slices.

Remember when you couldn't turn? When you steered through corners instead of surfed them? Don't get cocky—one day you'll look back at what now feels like a perfect, graceful dance and wonder why you were kickboxing the trail.

You know turns, but you don't know *good* turns. Long after I could slash through simple turns with an adrenalized mix of control and abandon I still stuttered

EMERGENCY LANDINGS

Some riders never aim for the sky. That's okay, but all of us eventually find ourselves in an unintended jump. Even if you never hope to hop, try to remember these tips for safe landings.

* **Stay loose.** Keep your elbows and knees relaxed but slightly extended.
* **Level your cranks.** This gives you a stable platform to absorb the landing.
* **Move your butt up off the saddle and slightly rearward.** This pushes the rear wheel down to help it land first.
* **Keep the front wheel straight.** For some reason we all twist the handlebar when we're in the air.
* **Don't brace yourself against the impact when you land.** Absorb it by letting the bike come up to you.

through tight, right-angle turns. I fell on switchbacks. Off-camber turns—which slant to the outside instead of being banked to keep you in—pitched me into the woods. Even basic turns could get ugly if I entered with just enough speed to kick my tires loose—if I lost the slightest bit of traction I blew the whole deal.

As a novice, you learned to turn. Now it's time to learn how to do some cool tricks while you turn: how to hold a line when your tires skitter loose in a corner, how to finesse your way through tight angles, stick yourself to off-camber turns, and loop around switchbacks without taking a dive.

Slow-Turn Techniques

Sometimes the corner itself—not your speed—presents the challenge. This is true with off-camber turns, tight angles, and switchbacks. You'll have more success with these tricky turns if you navigate

them at walking speed or just slightly faster—at least until you dial in your technique. Here's how to do that.

✴ **Off-camber turns** are tough because they slant down in the same direction that your inertia wants to throw you. So your bike drifts to the outside of the turn, as if gravity suddenly started working sideways. You've probably tried beating this by riding a tighter inside line—this lessens the effect but doesn't eliminate it. (Besides, the tight inside line is way slower and more likely to tie up your bike when your front wheel begins turning more than your rear.)

Do this: Lean your *bike out* and lean your *body in*. This tilts the bike against the outward pull, while your body acts as a kind of pivot. Your bike makes the turn kind of like a dog running a half-circle on a leash. Exaggerate the position at first so you can feel the forces

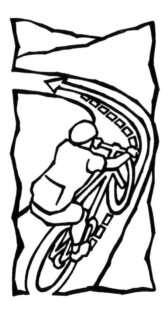

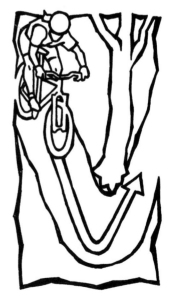

Stay on an off-camber trail by leaning your body—not your bike—into the turn.

Your rear wheel tracks inside your front wheel, so in tight turns ride a wide line to get both wheels through cleanly.

Ride straight to the apex of a switchback, point your front wheel out, and let go of the brakes.

that offset the pull; as you get better the movements will become subtler.

* **Tight turns** confound riders because we focus only on the front wheel—which completes the turn and seems to signal that everything is cool. Then the back wheel hangs up and we fall over. In a tight turn the rear wheel tracks inside the front wheel—and smashes against the inside corner. (If you don't understand this, ride an imaginary turn as tight as you can in sand or wet grass then go back and look at your tire tracks.)

  To get all of your bike through the turn, use this flight path (it pulls you far enough outside to keep your rear wheel from colliding with the inside corner): Steer your front wheel toward the *outside* of the turn—so much that it looks like you won't make the corner if you maintain the line. As the wheel reaches the outside edge, turn the handlebar sharply inside until the wheel points at the corner's exit. You got it.

* **For more control in tight turns,** try pedaling against the pressure of lightly applied brakes. (When you were a novice you learned to never brake in a corner. This is one of those advanced exceptions.) You'll see that you can control the tightness of your line with brake pressure. More brake = tighter line; less brake = wider line. This technique is especially useful when rocks or other obstacles dot a tight turn. You can steer your front wheel outside the rock and your rear wheel inside, then laugh like a fiend when your friends clear the rock with their front wheel but smash into it with their rear.

* A trail makes a **switchback** when it turns so sharply that it ends up running parallel to itself—kind of like a hairpin turn. Trail builders (and animals) blaze switchbacks when the slope is too steep to run the trail straight up or down. The technique for riding switch-

backs is similar to the tight-turn maneuver, but it's harder to do because you're losing (or gaining) elevation as you're turning. The stakes are higher.

It's less intimidating—and less painful—to learn the correct line by climbing switchbacks, so try that first. As you enter the switchback, go wide, where the pitch is less severe. At the apex, cut your front wheel sharply inside and point it toward the exit. Then jam on the pedals and your rear wheel should follow.

Descending switchbacks is more fun, more impressive, and more dangerous to learn. You'll fall. Everyone falls. Because you're falling to a surface that slopes away from you, the fall is long, but aside from scrapes and achy fingers, knees, and elbows, there usually isn't much damage because you're moving slow.

Use the same line you used to climb the switchback. Feather your brakes; go wide. At the apex, aim your front wheel out of the turn and let go of the brakes. Your wheel will pull you through the turn. That's all there is to it, but it's hideously hard to learn. Be patient and stay limber.

Really good riders get through switchbacks by riding inside and slightly past the apex and then yanking on the front brake, which pulls the rear of the bike up into a nose wheelie (a front wheelie instead of back), and swinging the back of the bike around so they can ride straight out. This is cool down to the soul, but impossible. Don't attempt it until you can do other impossible things.

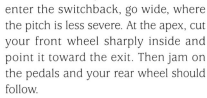

honing slow turns

- Lean your *bike out* and your *body in* on off-camber turns.
- To get through tight turns, steer the front far outside, then turn sharply and aim across the turn for a wide exit.
- For more control, pedal against lightly applied brakes.
- Use a wide entrance/wide exit pattern on switchbacks, climbing, or descending.

High-Speed Turns

Before we get into this, know three things. First, unless you really know what you're doing, skidding in a turn is slower than a controlled, full-traction coast. Second is the official bonehead warning: Plowing up dirt isn't cool on public paths. It rips up the trail, increases erosion, and makes anyone who sees you imagine that you're a renegade extremist—living proof that trails should be closed to mountain bikers.

Third, on race courses or dirt or gravel roads (where the ecological and social consequences are nil), skidding through corners is one of the gnarly essences of mountain biking. You fly into a curve with more speed than you should, the tires start to slip sideways (you can tell from the

To corner with speed and controlled abandon, let your rear wheel drift, then hook it up by weighting the outside pedal and the wheel itself.

little shudder the bike gives), then they hook up and slingshot you out of the turn. You, my friend, are fire.

At first this technique will feel like a mistake to you. As a novice you taught yourself that when the wheels break loose it's a sign that you're doing something wrong, losing that magic traction. But with a high-speed slide—known as *wheel drift*—you control the slip so you can enter the turn with more speed than you could if you focused only on maintaining traction. Here's how.

* Experiment with wheel drift in a corner with a loose surface. As you ride through it, make your rear wheel slide by applying the rear brake. When the slide starts to feel too sketchy, let go of the brake and the slide will stop. That's not the technique—it's just to show you that you can slide without wrecking.

* Now go through the same turn, but instead of using the brake to start a slide do it with speed. (Remember: You don't want to use the brakes at all in a turn.) Go through faster and faster until your wheels break loose. This time, stop the slide by moving your weight back or weighting the outside pedal. That's the technique. It's called making your tires hook up.

* The ideal is to have both wheels break loose at the same time. If just the rear wheel slides, you're more likely to loop it around and wreck. If just the front wheel slides, you're in trouble—and into an even worse wreck. Make a sliding tire hook up by moving your weight where the problem is—back if the back is slipping, for instance.

* When both wheels start sliding, let the bike drift as long as you see that you'll still make the corner. When they drift far enough out, hook them up by weighting the outside pedal, and your bike will shoot you out of the corner at the last instant. It's really cool.

Narrow Minded

Staying on skinny singletrack is a miracle. Remember when you knew that? Railing the trail is one of those physical activities, like walking, that begins as an impossibility, then quickly—maybe too quickly for us to savor the freshness—becomes something ordinary.

This is why mountain biking is sometimes greater than life itself: Long after staying on singletrack becomes reflex (riding loose, focusing on where you want to go instead of on what you want to miss), the earth will wobble your world by throwing tightropes in your path. Even experienced riders can get the jitters on a narrow bridge or sidehill trail that cuts across a ridge or mountain, creating a sheer drop-off on one side.

As a novice you learned the basic techniques for tightroping—relaxation and anticipation—when you learned to stay on the trail. Rely on those instincts (they are instincts by now, aren't they?) but add three new tricks: Lean toward sideways drops, go faster to improve balance, and never hesitate on an approach.

A 2 × 4 in your backyard is an unforgiving—but not punishing—tutor. Ride that and you can ride where only the Wallendas would walk.

The Thin Cool Line

Here's how to take fat tires across skinny terrain.

* **Lean toward sideways drops.** On sidehill trails our instinct is to lean away from the drop—in toward the hillside, where we'll be safer if we fall. But this drags your inside pedal closer to the upslope, making you more likely to clip the earth and lose your balance. It also slowly pushes your bike's line outward—just where you don't want those wheels to go. Either lean your bike slightly toward the drop (so you're slanting inward while the tires follow a safe line in the middle), or keep your bike straight upright and lean your body outward.

* **Go fast enough to ride straight.** You have a speed at which your bike stops stuttering and settles into a smooth, straight-ahead line. Find that speed. That's how fast you should go on narrow trails. Slower—and wobblier—isn't safer.

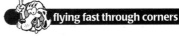

flying fast through corners

- Learn a controlled (braking) skid first.
- Initiate a true slide with speed, not brakes.
- To make the wheels hook up, weight the outside pedal (or move your weight in the direction of the sliding wheel—forward for the front wheel, back for the rear). Slide both wheels at once.
- Drift through the corner. At the apex, hook up the tires and shoot out of the turn.

It's counterintuitive and scary, but lean your bike toward the drop on a sidehill trail. Keep your body straight and you'll have balance, traction, and pedal clearance.

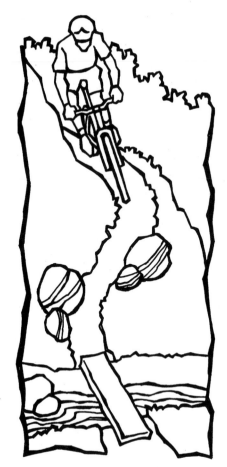

Stay steady on narrow surfaces by approaching with enough momentum to eliminate wobbles. Slower isn't always safer.

how to ride skinny things

- Lean your bike toward—not away from—sidehill drops.
- Carry enough momentum to ride without wobbling.
- Approach steady or stop before you get on the skinny part.

(Faster isn't, either, although it's usually more fun.)

* **Make a steady approach.** As you mount a bridge or sidehill singletrack, make a go or no-go decision before the scary, narrow part. Decisiveness is steadiness; indecision is a trip into the abyss. But don't panic if your entry isn't smooth and controlled. Just look ahead at how much room there is for your wheels. Don't look at how far you'll fall or how your knobs are hanging off the edge. Trying to dab—putting a foot down when there's barely room for your tires—

almost always ends up worse than riding through the wobblies.

Unbraking

The guy is the real thing, an old-school soul rider in a cotton T-shirt. Duct tape holds one of his gloves together. No bright decals in hip typefaces on his frame. But he can ride.

He rides like your dream of yourself, the bike an extension of his body, or his body an extension of his bike. His physical movements are small and fluid, but they explode into huge leaps and railed carves that hold the earth no matter how rugged the surface gets. His speed is not that of mountain bikes but motorcycles and cheetahs. You know all of this because you've thrashed yourself thoughtless chasing him down two miles of loopy, banked singletrack in Colorado.

I never found out the guy's name. Mainly because when he finally stopped at the base of the mountain and I caught him, I couldn't talk. I hung my head over the handlebar until I heard him start to ride off. I got out one question. Sort of.

"How so fast?" I asked.

He said, "Don't use brakes." And took off.

My brain was regaining enough function to understand abstractions such as resentment. Just as I began to resent his smart-ass impossible answer, the guy turned and said. "So much."

Comfort vs. Control

One of the reasons so many of us ride like beginners for so long is because we go too slow. I'm not talking about the lazy pace caused by fatigue or lack of fitness. I'm talking about how we scrub off speed when we shouldn't—when we are strong and the trail is open but still we slow ourselves by grabbing for the levers.

Our mental dashboards have two warning lights. The first one flashes when we exceed our comfort level. The second one strobes out big time when we pass our control level. But most of us never see that second warning. We stop at comfort, which means we never find the limits of our control. At the intermediate riding level that's where some of the most important learning happens.

Comfort rides are good for building confidence and for just enjoying the day. But if you never leave this zone you become an eternal beginner—slightly better than a first-timer, but not truly skilled.

I'm not suggesting you start riding with no brakes, just that you try riding without them on certain sections. Hold off one second longer before grabbing your levers; let them go one second sooner. Get closer to your limit of control—and then push the limit back.

Try these drills:

* Ride to a grassy field or empty parking lot. Without ever touching your brakes, ride around and see how long it takes the bike to slow or stop from certain speeds. Then see how you can affect the bike's movement by turning the handlebar, pulling the wheel off the ground, leaning to one side. You'll learn there are other ways to control a bike's flow besides using the brakes.

* Ride to a flat or slightly rolling technical singletrack. Try to ride a 20-foot section without using your brakes. You'll see how inertia keeps your bike rolling when the front end bunches up or when the rear hangs up after hitting obstacles. Now ride the same thing, dragging the brakes. The bike is less springy, more prone to stall instead of roll.

* Ride to a trail with rollers—short, steep rises—that max you at about 15 mph on the way down. Make sure the roll out is smooth, then practice riding up and over with no brakes. You'll begin to feel how a good singletrack draws the bike along—like a person swimming

with a tide instead of against it. When you use your brakes unnecessarily, you're fighting the tide.

Unbraking and Gyroscopics

Crested Butte biking guru Don Cook can box with the earth, but he prefers to dance. He has muscle-to-mass ratio to grind, but he floats. He's one of those people you want to ride like—grace and smoothness poured over fitness and experience. So when he grabs your rear wheel and tells you to get off your bike as he begins shaking it from side to side, you do. Without question. This must be a lesson. Or a fit of insanity inspired by years of focused riding. Either way, things should be interesting.

It is a lesson, about something Don calls "gyroscopics"—the importance of keeping the front wheel rolling.

"See," Don says as he cracks your bike from side to side, "with an unmoving rear wheel the bike can remain upright. But when you grab just the front wheel and shake the bike . . ." He does. "It falls." It does. "When the front wheel stops moving, staying up becomes much harder. Sorry about that gash in your saddle."

A ripped seat was worth the lesson. Don was talking about something subtler than momentum (which is about keeping enough speed to ride well). Gyroscopics aren't about how fast or slow you ride, but about letting the front wheel revolve at all speeds.

A rotating front wheel is more likely to roll through a tricky section than one clamped between brake pads. A rotating front wheel won't dig into the ground after a drop-off or a downhill log jump. A rotating front wheel pulls you through a switchback. It leads the bike across loose scut

ride fast and smooth . . .

- Hold off one second longer before depressing the levers; let them go one second sooner.
- Learn what movements affect momentum.
- Ride a technical section with no brakes, then with the brakes lightly dragging.
- Swoop down a short, steep hill without using the brakes.

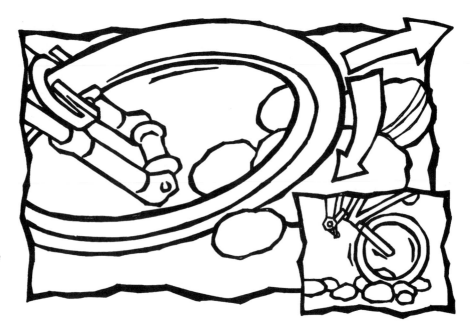

A rotating wheel has drive and stability. Stall your front wheel on obstacles, and you'll fall.

instead of demanding to be pushed. It finds ways over hub-high rocks.

Let your front wheel roll. It's not really a technique, but you'll find more stability, control, confidence, and rhythm if you remember it.

Funky Terrain

Gunnar Shogren is not riding, he's floating. And you're trying to hold his line at 23 mph, slamming across rocks and sliming over roots. He rolls while you rock, but you hang on, trying to live like a pro, even if just for a few seconds.

Shogren—a pro cross-country racer who grew up riding the technical trails of the East Coast—passed you just as you crested a two-mile climb on a race course in West Virginia's Monongahela National Forest. You caught a wheel and hung on because you just don't get many chances like this. The speed is not human, the lines are not humane. But Shogren is smoothness and small movements. He is levitation. You are an earthquake on wheels.

I talked to Gunnar after that race. I

wanted to know if he even remembered the section that I'll never forget. He did. He even admitted it was hard for him. But he knew how to float when the terrain got funky. That's why the section was hard for him but punishing for me.

Flotation Advice

There's no such technique as floating. It's a sensation you want to achieve whenever the ground gets weird. Sometimes you float by letting your bike bob beneath you. Sometimes you float by digging the wheels into loose terrain or getting them to hook up on wet slopes. Here's how to handle strange surfaces.

ROCK FIELDS
* Get up off the saddle, flex your knees and elbows.
* Pick out a line with big, embedded rocks that won't roll around under you like the small, loose ones will. But don't aim for boulders.
* If all you have to ride on is loose rock, sit way back and pin the stones under

"Smooth out" rockfields by using a muscly gear instead of spinning, and drive the rear wheel steadily.

your rear wheel. You'll get decent traction this way, but it wastes a lot of energy and makes your front ride light and twitchy.

★ Set up so you will enter and exit in as straight a line as possible. You might not be able to turn once you're in the rocks.

★ If you have to steer, do it by shifting your hips—but don't start juking. Stay centered over the bike and keep the front wheel straight.

★ Roll fast enough to let momentum smooth out most of the bumps.

★ If you have to pedal, use a gear that feels somewhat muscly instead of one that emphasizes fast spinning. This helps drive the bike into the ground. It also keeps you light on the saddle.

★ Keep the rear wheel driving. Propulsion will solve lots of problems and save you when you go off course. Give yourself one extra pedal stroke before you bail and you might not need to.

★ Let the pedals bang. You will hit rocks, the bike will bounce, but you will stay upright. Don't panic when pedal meets stone.

★ Don't freak if the rocks are wet. The only places traction disappears is on moss or when a lot of riders have tracked mud and slime onto rocks.

ROOTS

Roots perpendicular to the trail are no problem—ride right over them. Even if they're wet you'll be okay if you can approach them at a right angle. But trees don't know about right angles—that's a human thing. Most roots cross the trail slanted, which means your wheels will slip sideways and dump you. This is most common with the rear wheel, most painful with the front. Ride slanty roots like this.

★ No brakes, never, ever. Not once. Your wheels will skate.

★ Carry enough momentum to clear the rooted section without pedaling. Torque is bad.

★ Loft the front wheel over the nastiest angles. Do small wheelies—pull the bar

Lift the rear wheel just long enough to hop slippery roots.

back more than up. You want just enough air time for your front wheel to clear the root.

* Hop the rear. You don't want to bunny-hop unless you'll clear the whole section, because landing on roots and staying upright isn't going to happen. But you can pick the rear wheel up just long enough to get over a root by lifting with your feet, twisting your wrists forward, and slightly shifting your weight forward.

* Stay with a slipping tire. Don't bail as soon as the bike gets a little sideways. If you don't clamp the brakes or stomp the pedals, your momentum might carry you past the sketchy section.

COMPRESSIONS

When your bike drops into ditches, dips, gullies, gulches, and other sharp-walled holes, you have to make sure the front wheel doesn't stick and the back wheel can scramble out after you.

* **To go through slow:** Shift your weight slightly back, level the cranks, and straighten your arms as you enter the hole, pushing the front of your bike down into it. As the bike bottoms, flex your arms and legs to pull the bike up into you and absorb the impact. Drive the front wheel out with a power stroke, then press down on it to maintain control. Shift your weight forward, and you're out. Don't touch the brakes at any time.

* **To go through fast:** Lift the front wheel by pulling it with your arms, shifting your weight back and giving a power stroke. When the front of the bike clears the hole, set it down on the other side and shift your weight forward so you don't crunch the rear wheel if it hits the side of the hole.

DROP-OFFS

You can ride your bike off sheer drops as high as two feet—higher if you have the guts to wheelie off the drop and land on your back wheel. If you're more conservative, do this.

* Shift your weight back as the front wheel approaches the lip. The steeper

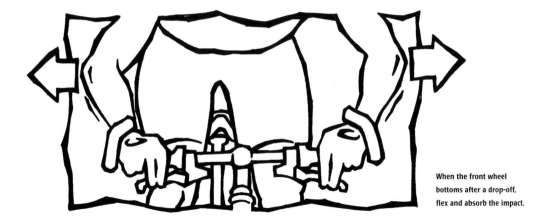

When the front wheel bottoms after a drop-off, flex and absorb the impact.

the drop, the farther back you move. On extreme stuff your butt will be hanging just over the rear wheel and your chest will stretch over the saddle.

✳ Extend your arms—without locking your elbows—as the wheel goes over. This pushes the bike off and down, and gets you in position to absorb the impact later.

✳ Keep a secure—but not clenched—grip to keep the wheel from turning sideways when it hits.

✳ When the front wheel bottoms, flex your elbows to absorb the impact. If you don't, all the shock will transmit into your body and you'll need ibuprofen after the ride.

✳ Shift your weight forward so you're not sitting on the rear wheel when it lands. You'll hesitate and stay too far back the first few times because you're afraid of moving forward and going over the bar. But once the front wheel has landed and begins rolling you won't endo.

✳ Center your weight after the rear wheel hits; bring your body back into the neutral ready position.

SAND

✳ As you enter a sandy area, shift your weight back to lighten the front wheel, then return to a neutral position when the whole bike is in the sand.

✳ Some riders get better drive by lightening the front wheel and digging the rear into the sand by shifting their weight back. Others—like me—prefer a centered position. Experiment.

✳ Keep the front wheel straight. Steer by banking the bike and leaning your body. If you turn the handlebar you'll sink into the sand. If you're totally bogged, however, you can quickly saw the handlebar from side to side and break free.

✳ If you don't mind wasting a lot of energy, shift down just before you enter, drop your elbows and pull back and down on the handlebar. You'll kick up a groovy roostertail and zing through the sand.

MUD

If you see mud, you probably shouldn't be riding. A wet trail is a tender piece of earth that your bike will violate. Avoid slopes that end in ponds or streams, trails where your tires leave tracks anywhere but in the low spots, trails where water collects or runs in your tracks, or if the ruts you leave will freeze or harden into erosion channels. And don't ride around puddles—you'll widen both the puddle and the trail.

On the other hand, some trails are eternally mucky and tougher than you or your bike will ever be. Those you can ride.

Float through mud by shifting your weight rearward and lightening the front just enough to keep it from digging in.

* Brake to a safe speed and slide rearward before you enter muck. If you come in too fast and heavy in the front, your forward wheel will deflect and pitch you into the mud, or dig in and flip you. Either way, you're in the mud.
* If you're a light rider, or if your natural pedaling style tends toward spinning, shift to an easier gear and try to prop through the water like a pedal boat. Use smooth strokes to maximize rear wheel traction and avoid dropping your body weight onto the wheels.
* If you're a heavy rider or a grinder, let your bike sink to the bottom of the mud and shovel-stroke your way through. It ain't pretty (neither is a plow horse), but it gets the job done.

WATER CROSSINGS

Eco-sensitive riders always walk through water. It leaves less trace of your passing and eliminates the possibility of some of your lube or grease getting into the water. I walk only when it looks like my tires might damage something—like moss or other vegetation—or if the water is so deep it'll suck the momentum from my bike and dunk me. That's usually about hub high.

If you coddle your bike you shouldn't ride through water that reaches your bottom bracket. Water and bearings are a bad mix. If you ride in water, do this stuff.

* Shift your weight back as you enter to prevent an endo or squirrely front wheel.

Splash, don't dive: Slightly unweight the front of the bike and paddle through water with fast but even pedal strokes.

❋ If you ride light or don't weigh much, shift your weight forward after you enter, centering yourself for better overall traction. Heavy riders should just sit and spin.

❋ Keep a fast but even cadence, and don't worry about trying to avoid rocks. If they're submerged they usually aren't slippery enough to make you fall. It's the semi-covered surfaces that get slick.

RUTS

Ruts that run across a trail are bumps—unweight and congratulate yourself on your expertise. But what's that up ahead? Why is that rut cutting down the middle of the trail? That is not good. It wants to eat you and your bike. Here's how to avoid becoming the earth's lunch.

❋ Level your cranks—or a pedal will catch the side of the rut.

❋ Don't try to steer out of a rut if the walls are higher than 4 inches: Your front wheel will lock against the wall or bounce off and thrash you around.

❋ Look for a section where the walls of the rut are shallow. Aim for that spot, then lift your front wheel out and lunge the rest of your bike clear. If your rear wheel doesn't make it out, let it skid sideways for a second, then lunge again.

❋ If you can't lunge out, settle in and ride the rut. Stay centered, stay calm, keep your pedals clear of the sides, and tell

When you're in a rut, level your pedals, don't try to steer out until the walls are shallow, and stop watching so much TV.

your friends it's not as bad as it looks. Maybe they'll believe you and drop in to share your horror.

WASHBOARD
This rippled surface is nature's corduroy—and just as fashionable. Washboard will rattle your kidneys and wear out your hands and arms in 30 seconds. But there's not much danger beyond blurry vision if you remember not to tighten up.

* Keep your grip secure but not clenched.
* Rise slightly off the saddle, bend your knees and elbows, and let the bike bounce beneath you. (Done right, your head should stay on about the same plane while the bike makes like a rodeo bull.)

* Slow way down for turns on washboard. Just as your tires hook up they'll hit the top of a ripple and skid.

STEPS
Riding steps—natural and manmade—is the coolest easy skill in mountain biking. It looks much harder than it actually is. To practice, find a set of eight or 10 steps. Any fewer and the ride is over before you know what happened.

* As you approach the first drop, shift your weight back.
* Let the bike bounce itself down—no arm pushes as in a drop-off.
* Don't turn the handlebar.
* Absorb the shock by flexing your knees and elbows. Each hit isn't very big, but

Steps are easy. Honest. Just
let the bike bounce down
and flex your body to soak
up the impacts.

because they come rapidly you'll need to work harder than you're used to.

* If you gain too much speed, feather the front brake to trim some speed. But going too slow is more dangerous than going too fast: If you stall you won't be able to get a foot down before you fall.

Speed Thrills

Speed scared me when I was a novice. I was a slow beginner, all intent on grace and smoothness. I convinced myself that after I learned how to ride—after I absorbed the fundamentals—I'd go faster. It worked.

I love the blur of green that's a forest at 30 mph. I love the way my eyes water,

how the trail smoothes out beneath my wheels at 25. I love the feel of flowers snapping against my thighs and the hole left in my body when my stomach doesn't follow me past the rim of a descent. I love speed.

But I wish I'd gone faster sooner. I have this friend Stan who started riding about the same time I did. He was my opposite—a heavy guy who rode hard and fast immediately, trusting pure speed to carry him over things for which he lacked technique. *Get the thrill, then the skill* worked for him. We're pretty much the same rider these days. But I think I'd be much better if I'd gotten an earlier start on riding closer to the edge.

We all begin our mountain-biking lives

boss

how to speed safely

- Look farther ahead than usual.
- Ride straighter.
- Control your bike with small movements.
- Ride loose.

at one of the two speed extremes—too slow or too fast. It's only when we become intermediates that we learn what we lack. If you're a slow finesser like I was, don't wait too long to start speeding; if you're a natural missile, spend some rides becoming a smart bomb.

A Quick Lesson in Control

Fast doesn't have to mean dumb or dangerous. You can test your limits and still walk without a permanent limp. Here's how to have a fast time you can live to talk about.

* **Extend your view.** The faster you go, the farther you look ahead. At walking pace I fix my vision inside five to 10 feet. On a long, open downhill, I'm focused almost on the horizon. How do you know what's right? Keep extending your view until the trail stops throwing surprises at you. You don't want to be like a car outrunning its headlights at night.

* **Ride straighter.** You don't need to bob, turn, weave, and writhe when you're a blur. Speed smoothes out the trail and lets you roll over things you'd have to maneuver around if you went slower. You're a speedboat skimming the waves, not a rowboat rolling in them.

* **Make smaller movements.** The faster you go, the subtler your body adjustments become. Just like an eagle in full dive, you can make a bigger swoop with a tiny flick at speed than you can with a big flap when you're going slow. This is why so many riders feel out of control when they're going fast—they're still making the big movements they learned at slow speed.

* **Ride loose.** At speed, it's more important than ever. Twitch your fingers, talk to yourself, lightly swing your elbows.

Speed Riding

Some of us think we're just not fast, and some of us think we're going about as fast as we ever will. We're all wrong. (Isn't that wonderful?) Here's how to unleash your own personal speed demon.

The faster you go, the farther you look. Never outrun your eyes.

how to go faster

- Spin the pedals faster, not harder.
- Do a few sprints on every ride.
- Use an aerodynamic position on smooth downhills.

For a surge of speed, pedal faster, not harder.

* **Learn to accelerate quickly.** Getting up to speed quickly means you can hold the high pace longer. It also helps you burst over rollers or sprint for the finish. Many riders try to accelerate by putting more power into the pedals. That's a leg blower. The more efficient way is to increase your *cadence*. Think *faster*, not *harder*.

* **Vary your speed in every ride.** We all have an average speed—the pace we ride most of the time. That's okay, but don't spend all your time at that speed. Toss a few sprints into each ride. The terrain guarantees that we'll work on climbing and descending every ride, but nothing forces us to speed, so the technique can get ignored.

* **Go aero.** Road riders know all about tucking—pulling in their arms and legs, dropping their heads and becoming a smooth shell for air to flow over instead of batter. Mountain bikers can't go aero as often. But tuck on a smooth downhill and watch your speed climb at least 3 to 5 mph. Just be sure that when you drop your head you keep your eyes on the trail.

Spin Cycle

Some of the coolest mountain-biking skills are the most subtle—like learning how to spin.

Spinning is different from pedaling. Most off-road riders are pedalers. They mash—stomping the downstroke and forgetting about the pedal on the upstroke. This wastes a lot of power because you're transmitting energy through less than half the pedal stroke. The uneven power output also decreases your traction (because the rear wheel isn't being driven steadily) and causes the bike to sway (messing with balance and control).

Try *pulling up* on the pedals next time you ride. If the sensation feels funky, or if just a few minutes of it fries your legs, you're not a spinner. But you can be.

The goal is an impossible one: to spin circles. Studies have shown that not even the best riders can deliver consistent amounts of energy up and down through an entire stroke. There are always dead spots. But if you strive for circles you'll end up with a fuller stroke than with the up-and-down mash. Here's what to do on your next ride:

* Push down. (Simple, huh?)
* Just before the pedal reaches the bottom of its stroke, pull back on it as if you're trying to scrape mud from the sole of your shoe.
* Pull up.
* Just before the pedal reaches the top of its stroke, push forward on it.

You'll end up with a stroke that resembles a square more than a circle, but remember to *think* circles. It helps. If you

think square, you mash. Practice with one leg at a time for just a few minutes. You'll fatigue quickly—when you do, switch the effort to the other leg. When the second leg dies, forget about spinning and just ride. In a few weeks you'll be a spinning fool.

When I teach this technique, some riders always ask if they'll concentrate so much on the cross and upward motions that they forget to push down hard enough—actually resulting in a weaker all-around stroke. Nope. Your legs have muscle memory that takes care of the downward force.

The Cadence Question

The idea of spinning seems to imply that your legs are superhuman blurs. Someone's always asking me how many revolutions per minute they should spin. I don't know. Really. Numbers geeks know that staying between 65 and 100 rpm is the most efficient range for most riders. But what happens when you're on a muddy hill and you need to pause your stroke to time out the approach to a log hop? What happens in loose gravel—where you want to muscle out a harder gear for better drive and traction? There's no optimal rate for mountain biking.

That said, I think most novices and fresh intermediates spend too much time spinning slowly—somewhere between 40 and 65 rpm even on easy, flat stuff. Check your cadence on your next ride; if you're low, spend some time at higher revs. Watch better riders and try to match their gearing and cadence.

The best way to pick your cadence has nothing to do with numbers. It's based on your body: If your lungs are tired, slow your cadence; if your legs are tired, speed it up.

Crash Course

The guy with a Barbie head wired to his handlebar screams, "If you ain't bleedin',

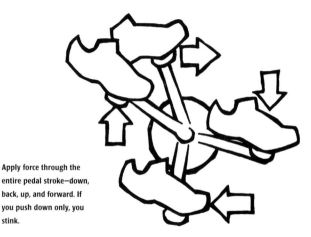

Apply force through the entire pedal stroke—down, back, up, and forward. If you push down only, you stink.

you ain't speedin'," and raises his hand for a congratulatory high-five that you would return if you could lift your arm above your shoulder. Instead, you give him a sick little smile, half pain and half pride.

Your forearm is hamburger. A piece of your elbow shines white through a ragged red corona. Gravel sticks out of your bicep. Although somehow you rode five miles after your bike slid sideways down one of Washington's Cascade Mountains, you won't be back on two wheels again for a month.

But you will be back. You know that even as the scrub brush—wielded by someone else because you could never do this to yourself—opens up nerve endings as it sandpapers the grit out of your wounds. You will always be back, despite the wrecks. Maybe, in a weird way, because of them.

Falling and Love

Mountain bikers—even the tamest of us—savor the danger of the sport. Grandparents taking my riding clinics proudly point out their scratches to their family afterward. I've thought about this a lot—usually while I'm lying on my back waiting to see which part of my body hurts—and I believe we can embrace the danger because mountain biking actually is a pretty safe sport.

Most wrecks are scratch-and-rides or simple bruisers. Minor biffs. Even something as spectacular as an endo or face-plant usually results in nothing more than abrasions or sprains. But in mountain biking, the Big One—like my slide down the Cascades—is always out there, waiting. Our little diggers remind us of that and, despite what anyone says, there's a hell of a rush in that feeling.

I'm not saying you need to become one of those boneheads who shows off scars at a dinner party. But—especially if you're middle-aged and all responsible

INTRODUCING THE PEDAL RATCHET

Before your pedal collides with an obstacle, ratchet it back up and give another small stroke to maintain momentum.

While you're practicing your spin, play with another helpful pedal technique: the ratchet. You use a ratchet when the trail surface is jagged and high enough to catch your pedals on the downstroke—as you pass by a series of rocks, for instance.

Instead of pedaling a complete downstroke, stop about halfway down, pull your pedal back up and repeat the motion. With this technique you can propel yourself long distances without trapping your pedal against jutting obstacles.

and settled and stuff—don't be ashamed when you're compelled to share your crash stories. You're alive and happy about it. That's cool.

Of course, the best way to enjoy this funky affection (affliction?) is to keep the really nasty wrecks to a minimum.

Most of the advice in this regard is so stupid—Use Caution on Unfamiliar Trails—that if you don't already have it figured out for yourself you're too dumb to follow advice anyway. Other things people say are impractical (like most of us really have the ability or reflexes to tuck our heads down, round our shoulders, and execute a karate roll to avoid injury during an endo). Some advice is good theory that we'll ignore because we're human (like not letting our bikes outspeed our skill—sure, until I start having fun).

Turn a crash into a controlled roll by pulling in your limbs. Good luck.

What people in my riding clinics most appreciate are a few simple tips on how to bail.

* **Don't stick stuff out.** When a tree falls, the branches are pulverized but the trunk is peachy. Don't snap your branches—try to land with your trunk. Experts advise curling into a ball, but I've never been able to do that. Instead, I just don't extend my limbs—no bracing myself against the impact with outstretched arms, no attempts to catch myself with hands and fingers. I thud but I don't snap.

* **Don't skid—roll.** Don't worry about becoming a safe little ball. It's great if you can do that, but the most important thing is to go with your momentum. When you skid you create a lot of skin-frying friction and are more likely to snag a limb on something. When you roll you travel farther but lighter. The exception: When you're riding cliffs or steep slopes,

skid. I once rolled within half a foot of a hundred-foot drop.

* **Stay with your bike when possible.** Unless you're launched, hang on to the handlebar, stay clicked in, and the strong-and-brave bike frame will take most of those nasty impacts. (But don't come running to me if this backfires and a bar-end breaks a rib or something.) Staying with your machine is almost always safer. Almost always.

* **Let your bike run away if you can bail backwards.** You look funny when you do this, but you don't get hurt, so who cares. When you lose control on a downhill or flat, just slip off the back of your bike and let it roll away. Hit the ground with your feet moving and run yourself to a stop.

* **Cover the largest chainring.** On descents you're supposed to shift onto the middle or big ring to stop the chain from slapping against your frame or derailing. Choose the big ring whenever you can. Your chain takes the edge off the ring's teeth, which your leg will appreciate if you go down.

 how to wreck safely

- **Land on your trunk instead of your limbs—don't stick out your arms or hands.**
- **Roll, don't skid.**
- **Stay with the bike when possible.**
- **Slip off the back if you lose control on a descent.**
- **Put the chain on your big ring.**

RIDING ON THE EDGE: EXPERT SKILLS AND BEYOND

Have you become as good a mountain biker as you're ever going to be?

That's a question I ask myself every few weeks, usually after I've taken my favorite hometown trail in a fluid, no-dab dance. One day you'll ask yourself that same thing—maybe you already have. By the time you're a good enough rider to know such a question exists, you'll also anticipate the answer.

Technically, we will never stop improving. There will always be one more refinement to a technique, one more small moment of wasted motion to eliminate, one fraction of a fraction in jump height to gain. But, realistically and practically, we all reach a point where significant leaps in skill are history.

I'm going to be about the same rider I am now for the rest of my life. Not that a quantum change is impossible. It's just that I'd have to slice off a huge chunk of my regular life and devote it to cycling—and that's coming from someone who rides nearly every day. The greatest riders *live* the sport. I know mountain bikers who ride twice a day and miss their bikes in between. Maybe you'll become one of those. Or maybe, like me, you'll stop somewhere just before the peak—still high enough so that you can barely see where you started, but low enough to always make you wonder how far you could've gone with absolute devotion (and no other life).

Anyone with moderate fitness and regular access to a mountain bike—as little as twice a week—can become an intermediate-level rider. Only a few can leave the crowd behind. And only you can decide where you'll top out. You probably don't even know yet. You'll have a better idea once you begin testing yourself against expert-level skills. Most of the gains that remain are small in result but mammoth in effort—not worth the trouble to many people.

There are still some giant leaps waiting for you—like the trick jumps explained in this chapter. The ideal that I think has the most influence on our evolution into expert mountain bikers is riding with *style*.

Personal Style

Great riders have style—not flashy movements or cool clothes or attitude, but a way of riding a bike with presence. You can see their style in small motions most people never notice—little shifts of the hands and feet, a way of breathing steadily even after their lungs incinerate, the way they sit on a saddle.

These motions and postures aren't important, but what they're telling you is. Great riders have an idea of how they want to ride—call it a philosophy—and this idea affects and elevates every action they make on a mountain bike.

Style is hard to define—but it's easy to spot. The great world-champion downhiller Missy Giove has it. She's even talked about it, although she doesn't call it style. She calls it flow. "Attaining a flow state—that's your goal when descending," Giove says. "I hit it every ride, sometimes for the whole ride, sometimes just for part. Let it come and take you."

That's her style: Attain flow. She'd have been good without that style—certainly better than most of us, and perhaps even great. But she never would have become a world champion. Without a style of your own you'll never be great. You'll be good, perhaps very good, but merely good.

Here are two other styles—or philosophies—I admire. Copying style is not style, but maybe you can make one of these the starting place for developing your own.

* **Ride like water.** Paul Adkins is a guide for West Virginia's Elk River Touring Center, and he's outwitted death on harrowing rides across Alaska. He's one of the smoothest riders I've ever seen. He says, "Flow like water down a

mountain, simply and instantly following the path of least resistance. As water finds the smoothest line, sometimes around rocks and logs, sometimes over, so should you. To do this you need to relax so completely your mind enters a state of extreme focus and concentration. You're totally engulfed by each moment in time, using 100 percent of your mental capabilities, but the trick is you're not using this mental focus to solve riding problems, you're using your brain to relax your brain. If you can do that well enough the problem-solving ride part of your mind will hum along in the background, doing all the things you need to do smoother and faster than you could do them deliberately.

"One of the techniques I use to get into this focused state—it sounds stupid but it works—is that I repeat this phrase over and over while I ride: 'Float like a butterfly, sting like a bee, make this trail as smooth as can be.' Say it over and over and over and over and over, and it takes your mind off your hurting legs, off the fear of flipping over the bars, off everything."

* **Don't be at war with the earth.** Bob Roll is a pro cross-country mountain-bike racer who began his career as a roadie riding in the Tour de France, Paris-Roubaix, and other classic events. He says, "Mountain biking shouldn't be based on the idea of overcoming and conquering, or else paying for your failure to do so. Mountain biking should be freed from conflict so your riding becomes a means for personal expression. The more you cease seeing trails as problems to be solved the more you will transcend the forces of gravity and mechanics. When you fully disconnect, the trail will look different. There will be no 'obstacles.' You'll see it like a canvas or piece of paper on which you can express yourself."

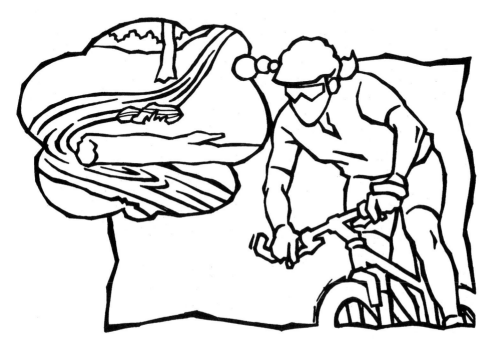

Ride like water: Flow along the path of least resistance.

Jumping for Joy

One day you will go too fast, launch off your favorite jump and feel the rear of your bike kick to one side. It's a natural counterforce to the body lift that helps pull you into the air. It feels cool, a little moment free from gravity.

It looks cool, too. You know that because you've seen other riders do it—pros playing to a crowd, full-page photos in bike mags, and that local hotshot showing off. Next time you jump you'll draw the kick out a little more, let the bike heel over mid-flight, and maybe even tilt a

When you jump, your rear wheel naturally kicks to one side. Just don't land like this.

shoulder. You'll wreck, if not this time, then the next. Or the next. Soon, anyway. You won't be able to pull the bike back under you, and you'll land with your frame leaning at a crazy angle or with the front wheel crossed up.

If you kick your bike out the next time you catch air after that wreck, then you know you're ready to start jumping with flash. Even though the earth reminded you that you must pay, you're ready to play.

Pumped to Jump

Mid-air tricks stretch out your perception and enjoyment of a jump. The sensation of soaring increases—and so does your understanding of how to move the bike beneath you on the ground. Trick jumps not only make you cooler, they make you better.

One of the first moves you'll do is a big *kickout*—snapping the rear to one side (it will go one way naturally) with your hips, then pulling it back underneath you before you land. There's not much technique to learn, just timing. A lot of riders also cross the handlebar up—turn it sideways in the opposite direction of the kickout. Again, it's all timing.

Another cool, basic aerial trick is to bring the front of the bike up toward your chest, so you appear to be doing a wheelie in midair. You can push the front back down with your arms, or tap your rear brake while you're flying. This changes the dynamics of your bike's movement, not only dropping the front wheel but making you look like you're momentarily motionless. (Never touch the front brake while you're in the air.)

The 360—a complete turn—is

Pull a 360 by hopping, then swinging your head into the turn and pivoting your hips.

doing trick jumps

- Accent your bike's natural kickout.
- To create the illusion of pausing during a jump, bring the front of the bike up toward you in midair, then drop it. You can push it back away from your body or tap the rear brake.
- Learn to do a 360 on the ground by hopping in place. Practice on a jump no higher than a curb.

the classic trick jump. You learn this first by doing 180s from a standstill on level ground. Hop in place, then swing around by swiveling your head into the turn and your feet out of the turn. Pivoting your hips helps both motions. Be sure to turn in the same direction your bike kicks when you jump.

When you can do a complete circle, you're ready to try it off a small jump—no higher than a curb. Go slow and expect to wreck. Doing a 360 off higher and longer jumps is actually a little easier (as long as you've practiced completing a circuit and landing on short, small jumps) because you can spin slower.

How to Not Jump

Jumping is great for the soul, terrible for speed. Every time your bike loses contact with the ground it also loses some momentum. The closer to the earth you stay, the faster you go.

When speed is what you need, here's how to stay grounded and still smoke

How to Hop in Place

Before you can learn 360s you need to be able to hop when your bike is at a standstill. Your first attempts will feel awkward—you won't be able to pull up both the front and rear of the bike simultaneously. Here's how to hone the standing hop.

* First, learn to rock your bike. Weight the front wheel then pull it up as you would for a wheelie. As you let the wheelie down, shift your weight forward, pull up with your feet and twist your wrists to pull the back wheel up. As you let the back down, pull another wheelie. Repeat the sequence, trying for a faster rate of rocking. Locking both brakes throughout the rock will help you balance the bike.

* When your rock is steady and swift, try to eliminate the dead spot in the middle of the motions and combine the front and rear lift. Get it right and you've done a hop.

* A smoother way to hop is by lifting the entire bike at once instead of with two (front and back) movements. Just compress your body into the bike and spring upward. You can twist your wrists for more rear lift. This is probably how you'll end up hopping once you dial in the technique, but rocking is easier to learn.

Learn how to hop in place by rocking your bike and then combining the two lifts into one motion.

* The expert step is to combine your hops until you can pogo in place for long periods. This is a technique mainly used by trials riders in competition, but you can use it on the trail to line up for obstacles or simply to show off. When you try to do several hops in a row, one end of your bike—probably the front—will swing to one side. Don't panic, just pull the bike back under you with the next hop. With practice you'll be able to hop the bike around in a circle.

rollers, bumps, or other rounded obstacles. (Jump over anything with sharp edges or no ramped approach—you don't want to hit those with your wheel.)

Dead Jumps

This technique is kind of like wrecking into an obstacle on purpose—except you recover by absorbing the impact with your body. To dead jump you hit a bump at high speed and suck up the shock with your arms and legs. It's the same principle you learned when you were a beginner, except the force you're absorbing is one that would've broken you into tiny pieces back then.

* Approach the bump with your butt grazing the saddle.

* Just before you hit, extend your arms without locking them and move your butt behind the saddle (over the rear wheel).

* When you hit, let the bike come into your chest. Absorb the impact with your legs and arms. Because your butt is out of the way, the bike can travel about twice as far up into your body without causing you to lose control.

* As soon as you clear the crest, push the bike back toward the ground. The sooner you get back down the softer the landing and the higher the speed you'll have maintained over the section.

* Keep your butt back until you feel fully in control. If you move forward too soon, the rear can catch air when it hits the bump and fling you over the bar at high speed.

Speed Wheelies

This technique takes more timing but is slightly faster and smoother because the wheels get back to the ground quicker. There's less danger of getting flung over the bar on the back of the bump, but if you mis-time the wheelie you get smashed by an impact you can't absorb, or your bike stops short and you don't.

* As you approach the bump, do a wheelie. (There's no way to tell you when to start the wheelie, since that depends on how long you can ride one, how fast you're going, and the height of the bump. Try a few slow ones to gain experience in judging those factors.)

* At high speed, don't put too much force into pulling the wheelie—with the bike's momentum you're more likely to jack the front up so high you flip backwards.

* As soon as the front wheel clears the crest, push it down onto the backside of the bump. The sooner you get it grounded the faster you'll go—the back of the bump is like a little downhill, and the longer you're on it the more acceleration your body weight creates.

* Don't brace against the pedals, which will rise toward you when the rear wheel hits the transition. Let them come up into you. If you don't, the rear of the bike will toss you over the bar. This impact is easier to absorb than that of a dead jump.

Maximum Braking

Brakes were made to slow bikes, not stop them. That's something you realize when you make the leap from novice to intermediate—brakes are for control instead of panic.

When you become an expert mountain biker you realize that your levers don't only control your bike's speed—they also can be used to affect your line, to control your handling.

Actually, just the back brake gets this special job. The powerful front brake exists solely to slow your bike—as you become a better rider you'll rely more and more on

Keep your speed high over bumps by doing a dead jump instead of a leap. Let the bike stay grounded and buck up into your body.

Complete a speed wheelie by pushing the front down after it clears the crest. Keep pedaling. (This is fast.)

the front to scrub off speed. By learning to get your weight back quicker and smoother you'll be able to counteract higher and higher front-brake forces without losing control or flipping over the handlebar.

With more of the slowing power transferred to the front brake, you can begin using the back brake to maneuver. If your momentum is carrying you into a line you don't want, tap your rear brake as you simultaneously throw your weight to one side. Your bike will shoot to that side, leaping lines like a derailed and then magically re-railed train.

Play, Not Mush

Many expert riders set up their levers so there's some play—the lever depresses slightly before the pad hits the rim (or disc) and begins braking. This is to prevent fatigue and allow the fingers to stay on the levers without accidentally engaging the brakes.

But play doesn't mean mush: Once the brake pad hits the rim there should be no squishiness. The brakes should be solid the instant they're on. It's a pro setup.

There's no swerve in this technique, and no long lean required like there would be if you did a weight shift without the braking (the way you learned to change lines). The movement is a snappy, precise switch to a parallel line.

At slower speeds, and with smaller weight shifts from only your hips and feet, you can get the rear wheel to skip left or right. This is handy for changing the angle of your bike (instead of the whole line) when you're aiming for a turn or a clean path around an obstacle.

When Feet Are Faster

Sometimes your goal is to ride everything. You want to find out how far, how high, or how freaky your skills can take you. But today your friend is stuffing you—leaping out of the saddle to jam the hills, laying the bike into corners at warped angles to hold every bit of speed, shifting up for big-ring mashing on the flats.

The last of your spit has dried on the corners of your mouth. You can feel your leg muscles squirming against your skin like they want to get out. You've been beaten by the better rider. And then you see it: a freshly fallen tree trunk waist high right across the trail. Way too big to jump. Way too low to ride under. There's a blip in your friend's pedal whirl for the first time all day.

You streak toward the tree without braking, flip your right leg over the top tube, hit the ground running, slap the bike on your shoulder and vault that wooden barrier, then slide smoothly back onto the saddle and snap the pedals around. About two seconds have passed. Next time you look back you can't even see your friend.

Jump to a new line by tapping your rear brake just as you swing your weight sideways.

The Good Dis

When speed matters, hit your heels. Running dismounts are the quickest way to get over unrideable obstacles, through sections you're not sure you can ride, or across terrain you know you could ride if you went slower. Even if you can't pull a two-second pro-style dismount and re-entry, running with your bike is safer than risking a crash (and losing major places) in a race. The keys to running cool are the transitions.

☀ Once you have the technique dialed in, you'll approach the obstacle at normal riding speed—this is why it's quicker than slowing to ride or stopping to dismount. Until then, approach at walking speed.

☀ Pick your dismount spot before you get there. Remember, mountain biking is about anticipation. You need enough room to take at least two steps, probably more.

☀ Get off your bike. Unclip your right foot and swing it over the top tube. (You can swing it behind your bike—over the saddle—but your legs won't be in as good a position to run.) Bring your foot between your left leg and the frame. As you're doing this, unclip your left foot. When your right foot hits the ground, start running. It's much easier than it sounds, but practicing with running shoes on grass is a good idea.

☀ Shoulder your bike. As your right leg steps through, pick up the bike with your right arm. Most riders reach

do a running dismount

- Learn at walking speed.
- Unclip your right foot and swing it over the top tube.
- Unclip your left foot as your right leg comes over; start running when your right leg hits the ground.
- Shoulder the bike.
- Leap the obstacle.
- Take a few steps, then roll the bike beside you.
- Hop up with your left foot, swing your right leg up and over the bike from behind.

through the frame, grab the handlebar to prevent swinging, and rest the top tube on the shoulder. Some riders let the tip of the saddle rest on their shoulder. Others reach over the top tube and grab the down tube, carrying the bike under the arm like a briefcase. You'll find a position comfortable for you.

* Zip over that baby. Well, clamber over it, anyway.

* Take a few steps, then bring the wheels to the ground and get the bike rolling beside you. Put both hands on the handlebar and jump onto your bike by hopping with your left leg and swinging your right up and over from behind. It's important to come down on the saddle with the inside of your thigh instead of your crotch. You must understand why.

1: Unclip your right foot and swing it over the top tube.

2: Unclip your left foot and grab the bike as you begin running.

3: Shoulder the bike and vault that baby.

THE BALLISTIC BALLET: TRAINING AND RACING

Even people who aren't competitive should race at least once a season—at least once in a lifetime—to feel the intense focus of a race, the purity of intent and ignorance of consequence. A race cuts you open like a razor at the start, then, right at the end, heals you and leaves something extra inside. A race exposes your ugliness and magnifies your beauty.

There's also no better way to become a better mountain biker. Forget books (including this one), magazines, videos, helpful friends, and even years of recreational riding. Race and you will become better, stronger, faster, and smarter, no matter what.

Your First Race

You know this is a tough race. Just to get to the start at the West Virginia Fat Tire Festival you had to climb a mile on a dirt road, cooking under a summer sun that was closer to you than the top of the mountain seemed to be.

Then you packed yourself into the nervous, bouncy ball of color and odors that was your opponents. Standing room only under the start banner. This is it—the first start of your first race, and even though you don't know it now you'll never quite get used to this part.

The start of a race—any race—is every-

thing that is terrible and beautiful about mountain bike competition. Everything else that happens in a race can be sampled in some way when you're just out riding—dicing with friends, getting into a flow that pulls you along faster than you've ever been, somehow keeping your legs churning when you are empty. But a start is a ballistic ballet you can experience only in a race. The start isn't the best part of a race, certainly not the most beautiful or most rewarding, or even the most fun. But it's something that belongs only to racing. That's why every mountain biker should taste it at least once.

You're straddling your bike, shoulder to shoulder with everyone, someone is making jokes you can't quite hear, and someone else shouts to someone else about last week's race. And then the gun snaps. Or some guy holding a clipboard screams. You're caught in a gush of bikes and people and you're all breathing dirt, and the sound of shoes clicking into ped-

Every mountain biker should race at least once—it's the quickest way to get stronger, faster, and smarter.

als is like a brick of firecrackers going off. Someone's bar-end jabs your butt; someone else's handlebar hooks under yours. You stay upright only because there's no room to fall. Your elbow flicks out and digs into someone's soft side and you press the rider away.

From behind there's a shout shriller than the others—something besides or beyond joy in the sound—followed by the long scrape of bikes across the ground and the shorter, softer thud of bodies hitting dirt. It's a big pileup, maybe 10 bikes, and suddenly the pack loosens and gets faster. Your heart has never beat so fast or forcefully, and the air you suck in scorches your lungs. Everyone is faster than you, everyone is in your way, and you gasp for breaths so hard you stretch the corners of your mouth until they sting. You have never been happier on a bike.

The Racing Scene

One of the greatest things about mountain-bike racing is its accessibility. There's no snobbiness, no elitist barriers, no cliques. Racing is a festival, not a private party. Show up on the cheapest bike in a T-shirt and running shoes and you find yourself riding the same course as the sport's greatest pros—no stadiums or courts here. You share singletrack with people you've only seen in pictures, and those people talk to you as you ride. You know why? You're one of them.

Even though mountain-bike competition isn't an exclusive club, it can seem like one from the outside. Here's what you need to know to get in.

* **Races are divided into classes:** Beginner, Sport, Expert, Elite, and Pro. Beginner races are short—usually 4 to 10 miles. Some riders stay in the Beginner class for an entire season (or longer), but the Sport races are usually more fun. The courses are longer, more challenging, and more varied: You get more experience for your entry fee. There

are also a lot more riders—the Sport class has more participants than any other. I raced Sport my first time out (lots of people do it that way). But if you're nervous or you've never competed in any kind of bike race, try at least one Beginner event. Expert riders are honches; Elite riders are pros in waiting; Pros are gods.

You can upgrade from Beginner to Sport to Expert (or start in any class) at any time. If you finish well (top five in five races, for instance), you're automatically upgraded. To become an Elite rider, you apply to the national racing organization. Pro status comes when you win some Elite races and convince someone to sponsor you. If that's you, you're reading the wrong book.

* **Races are also divided by age:** Junior (18 and younger); Senior (19–34); Veteran (35–44); and Master (45 plus). In a race you don't compete against all the Sport riders or all the Seniors—you compete against the Senior Sports only. At large races the organizers sometimes divide the ages into even smaller categories, which is cool—and gives you a better chance at placing well.

* **There are also different kinds of competitions:** *Cross-country* races are usually run in laps that go up and down mountains, across lots of terrain changes. Everyone starts at once. *Downhill* races are like time trials—you go off alone, trying to beat the best time. Downhilling is becoming more and more popular but, unlike cross-country, you generally need a specialized bike—full-suspension designed solely for downhills—to compete seriously. In *dual-slalom* races, two riders start at once, weaving through a downhill course marked by flags. Miss a flag and you lose; beat your opponent and advance to the next round. In *trials* competition, you try to ride across a set course without putting a foot down or

wrecking. The rider with the fewest dabs wins.

* **You need a license to race**, but if you're just going to try a single event you get a special one-day license. A real license from the National Off-Road Bicycle Association (NORBA) costs about $30 a year.

* Besides the cost of a license, races generally have **entry fees** of $15 to $50. Sometimes you get a T-shirt or water bottle for entering. Prizes—usually parts or clothing—sometimes go as deep as the top 15, but more often only the top three to five win stuff.

* **You can find a race by looking in regional bike magazines or newsletters** (the national magazines can't list as many races) or checking with a bike shop. You might not know about any local races, but they're there. In fact, you'll be surprised how many there are.

Amazing Race

The best minds in cycling describe road racing as chess on wheels. Mountain-bike racing (at least at the amateur level) is more like a game of checkers played by extremely fit drunks—the tactics are brutal, simple, stupid, and someone always tips the board over before the end. In other words, a lot of the outcome is beyond tactical control because whoever's strongest wins.

Even so, there are some tricks that will let you steal a few places on the finish list.

* **Get there early for registration and sign-up.** The lines for these things would scare a Cold-War Russian grocery shopper. If you wait until attendance peaks you eat big chunks out of your pre-ride and warm-up time.

* **Pre-ride.** Ideally you get at least one full lap around the course so you'll know how long the climbs are (and how much effort you should put into each one), where the nightmare technical sections are (so you can finish with the same number of teeth you started with), where the singletrack runs (so you can get there before slower riders block you), where you can pass, where the food and water stations are, and all kinds of other useful things. Realistically, only the pros and serious amateurs looking to be pros get full pre-rides. The rest of us arrive late, chat with friends, forget our shoes. In fact, I've never fully pre-ridden a course. I like surprises and noble, bottom-half finishes.

* **At least try to ride some of the start**, then ride some of the course backwards from the end so you'll know when you're approaching the finish during the race. If there are any tough sections noted on the course maps you get when you sign up, sometimes you can cut across the course (instead of following it) to get a look at them.

* **Don't start cold.** You should arrive at the banner with some sweat staining your shiny new jersey, loose legs, and your heart primed so it won't have to make the leap from 60 beats per minute to 180. (It's much easier to hop from 120 to 180.) Do a 20- to 60-minute warm-up of moderate effort—you should be able to talk without panting while you warm up.

* **Choose your queue strategy.** Here's the deal: Line up under the banner early and you start from the front—but stand around 25 to 40 minutes getting cold. Warm up until minutes before the race and you start with 63 riders already ahead of you. If you're serious about a win, go early and take your chances—or have a friend try to save a spot for you. One good sneaky strategy: Go late and try to line up in about the fourth row, creating a new column on the outside of the pack. Sometimes it works. Sometimes people squirt

sticky energy drink at you until you leave.

* **Fill a spare tube halfway with air,** fold it four times and stuff it in your jersey pocket. This saves minutes if you flat during the race.
* **Load your hydration pack or water bottles with a mixture of half energy drink or fruit juice and half water.** Sometimes the aid stations have energy drinks, sometimes they just have water. Don't take chances. And don't think you'll have time to eat something solid.
* **Ride in control.** Novices get so amped up with adrenaline that they ride like pros for 50 yards, then explode into tiny pieces. If you've trained well you know your maximum pace—you'll go faster than that because that's racing—but try to stay close to your control level.
* **Pamper the downhills.** Everyone knows that descents are great places to make up time over wimpy riders. They're also the site of a sickening amount of carnage during amateur races. Better to finish slow than to perish fast.
* **Pick your opponents.** At the start, look for riders who appear to be about as fit as you are, ride about the same type of bike, and wear about the same type of equipment. These are your temporary enemies. Cherish them. Chase them. You will go faster.
* **Know the passing rules.** Don't try to pass when there's nowhere to pass. When riders behind you say, "Track," or "On your left," or "Ahem," let them by. If you block you're a doof. If someone blocks you, don't turn it into a war more important than the race itself. Wait until the course opens and go around.
* **Take extra clothes.** After the race you will lie on the grass wondering if you

are alive, rehashing the best bits with the people who finished with you, and admiring your muddy, bloody legs. But soon you will get chilly or feel the ooze begin to harden in the sun. You will want to become human again, and humans wear sparkly clothes. Besides, only posers model their filthy racewear hours after the thing is over.

Anatomy of a Plan

There's something beautiful about entering your first race completely unprepared for the physical Armageddon about to happen inside your body. Nothing else you do in life will ever hurt quite as much as it did before.

That's a great way to meet racing, but you wouldn't want to live there. As a novelty, suffering is cool. As a way of life, it sucks.

Besides, being fit for racing is even cooler than being a clueless novice with a fresh world waiting to be discovered. Being fit for racing means you rage. You are a hard thing, a fast thing. You are tight and springy and as invincible as a human ever gets. Your body and mind are armored with a shield built from miles of singletrack and hours of sacrifice.

When you're fit you do not race for entertainment like most people do. You race to race, and you will understand that if you devote yourself to training. You will understand it if, just once, you cross under a finish banner before anyone else, or climb atop even the lowest step on a podium with shoes still wet from mud, or even see your name in the top half of a results list stapled to a wall.

Honing your body the way you honed your riding skills can be so complex that it rules your life. Some people like it that way. But the process also can be as simple as setting rough weekly goals—a hillclimb one day, two speed workouts, a long ride, and a race.

Monitoring Your Heart Rate

If you're serious about training, you might want to invest in a heart-rate monitor to ensure you're on target—to benefit from intervals and recovery sessions you need to make sure your heart rate stays within certain ranges. You can guesstimate—max feels like the max, and at recovery pace you should be able to talk without panting. But nothing beats a monitor for ultimate accuracy.

If you get a monitor, first you'll need to determine your maximum heart rate so you know what your training ranges should be. (Example: If your max is 180 beats per minute, you'll recover at 60 percent, or 108 beats per minute.) To find your max rate, do a hillclimb that lasts at least 15 to 20 minutes at the hardest steady pace you can sustain, then sprint as you near the top. You should be at your max. A more scientific way is to mount your bike on an indoor trainer and do this test: Begin in your easiest gear. Maintain a cadence of 90 rpm. Shift up every 3 minutes until you can't maintain the pace. You've maxed.

Ignore the formulas (220 minus your age, 210 minus your age multiplied 0.65, etc.). They're bogus.

You probably should start somewhere in the middle and see where your inclination and lifestyle take you. Read through the descriptions for the three training programs in this section and decide which type of rider sounds most like you. These programs are excellent introductions to race training. There's no magic to them—they rely on the same elements all good training programs have, including the plans used by the pros.

The first element of a good training program is *endurance*, which is built with long, low-intensity rides. This is the easiest part of training because it mirrors how most of us ride before we begin training—casual rides at a casual pace. In fact, many people train too hard during their endurance workouts. If your muscles become sore or you breathe hard during most of the ride, you're going too fast.

The second element is *speed*, which develops from short, high-intensity efforts combined with structured periods of low effort or rest—the whole cycle is called an *interval*. Intervals hurt—you will hate them—but they raise the speed at which you can ride without pain (aerobically) and

improve your ability to ride hard even when your lungs and legs hurt (anaerobically).

The third element is *recovery*, which is more important than you might think. If your body isn't given time to regenerate, refuel, and heal, you won't benefit from all your hard work. Listen to the corny but profound cycling maxim: You don't get stronger from riding, you get stronger from resting.

Finally, there's *timing*. On a weekly scale, you must intersperse easy days and rest between your hardest efforts, and, ideally, sandwich an endurance ride between hard efforts so your body is adequately worked. The idea is to never do the same type of ride on consecutive days.

On a yearly scale, time your training so your fitness peaks for your biggest race. If you're reading this in November, don't dive into the training plans and expect to hold that intensity until a race in July. Generally, most racers work on building endurance through the winter, begin adding more speed workouts sometime between January and March, and hit full throttle by April or May. After the season—sometime between September and November—racers scale back their programs to minimal training and to riding just for fun.

Making the Plan Work

Even the best-designed training program is just an empty structure. It doesn't mean anything until you fill it with your sweat and time. You'll only be able to do that if you approach your training program with consistency and flexibility.

Consistency means doing the work as often as you can. You'll miss some days because of weather, work, family, friends, exploding bike parts, good television shows, and that extra beer last night. But the fewer workouts you miss—the more consistent you are—the fitter you become. Bottom line.

Flexibility keeps you from becoming

discouraged when you miss days or from getting stale when you never miss days.

When you blow a workout, don't imagine that your entire schedule is ruined. What's important is the week's effort. If you miss intervals on Thursday, do them on Friday and make Saturday an endurance day—skip that week's long, race-pace workout. Or skip the endurance ride. You'll eventually be able to feel which workouts are more important to your fitness. Training plans are suggestions, not orders. (Just be sure to always get enough recovery time.)

The other half of flexibility keeps you from getting burned out. After 10 weeks of 2-minute intervals you might want to do 10-minute hillclimbs instead; you might throw in a weekly ride to work on technical skills. Don't let yourself get bored. Bored people don't have dedication.

REST VS. RECOVERY

Rest means inactivity; recovery means an easier effort. You need both. Generally, recovery helps you more than rest—easy spinning will soothe your legs more than a day in bed will. But if you feel like your body has maxed out, opt for complete rest. Whichever you choose, make sure you drink plenty of water and refill your body with carbo on your rest/recovery days.

On with the Program

Here are the three training plans to get you started. You might not match one of the rider profiles exactly, but choose the one you most closely resemble. Remember to make the training program your own—that's key to long-term success—but if you've never trained for mountain-bike racing before, follow a plan closely for a month to give yourself a good reference for changes.

The up-and-comer can get fit in only 5 to 10 hours per week.

THE UP-AND-COMER

You ride three to six times per week, competing in one or two races every season. You haven't attempted much—if any—structured training. Most of your rides are 2 hours or less except on weekends, when you occasionally go for 3 hours or more. **Total weekly training time for this program: 5 to 10 hours.**

MONDAY
TIME: 60 minutes or less
GOAL: Rest or recovery (from weekend)

Spin in easy gears on flat terrain (55 to 65 percent of max), go for a walk with your dog, or take the day off.

TUESDAY
TIME: 60 minutes
GOAL: Short intervals

Warm up for 20 minutes at 55 to 65 percent of max. Do a series of all-out, 15-second intervals followed by 10 minutes of recovery. Do three of these, then cool down for 15 minutes.

WEDNESDAY
TIME: 60 to 120 minutes
GOAL: Endurance

Ride varied terrain at easy-to-moderate intensity (65 to 75 percent of max).

THURSDAY
TIME: 60 minutes
GOAL: Medium intervals

Warm up for 20 minutes at 55 to 65 percent of max. Do a series of efforts just below max—2 minutes at 85 to 90 percent—followed by 2 minutes at 60 percent. Go longer in the rest phase if you don't recover fully. Do three of these, then cool down for 15 to 20 minutes.

FRIDAY
TIME: 60 minutes or less
GOAL: Rest or recovery

Follow Monday's plan.

SATURDAY
TIME: 60 to 120 minutes
GOAL: Race or hard group ride

Race lovers compete up to once a month but haven't really focused on training yet.

If you don't race, do a ride that requires varied intensity but keeps you around 85 percent of max most of the time. You want to simulate a race pace.

SUNDAY

TIME: 60 to 120 minutes
GOAL: Recovery ride

After yesterday's thrashing, your body will recover better with a light workout rather than total rest. Ride easy terrain at 55 to 65 percent of max, going easier and shorter if you feel totally worked—just don't give in to the temptation to do nothing.

THE RACE LOVER

You ride four to six times per week, competing in four to seven races throughout the year—trying for one per month in peak season. You do some unstructured training—riding hard one day, then easy the next to recover—and push the intensity at least one day a week with friends who also race. You might do a couple 2-hour-plus rides a week, with one epic thrown in on weekends. You want at least one win this season. **Total weekly training time for this program: 6 to 11 hours.**

MONDAY

TIME: 60 minutes or less
GOAL: Rest or recovery (from weekend)

Spin in easy gears on flat terrain (55 to 65 percent of max), go for a walk with your dog, or take the day off.

TUESDAY

TIME: 75 minutes
GOAL: Short intervals

Warm up for 30 minutes at 55 to 65 percent of max. Do a series of all-out intervals of 10 to 15 seconds, followed by 5 to 7 minutes of recovery. Do four or five of these, then cool down for 15 minutes.

WEDNESDAY

TIME: 60 to 120 minutes
GOAL: Endurance

Ride varied terrain at easy-to-moderate intensity (65 to 75 percent of max).

The serious racer might train for two hours or more every day and wants to stand on a podium.

THURSDAY
TIME: 90 minutes
GOAL: Medium intervals

Warm up for 30 minutes at 55 to 65 percent of max. Do a series of 2-minute efforts just below max (85 to 90 percent), followed by 2 minutes of recovery at 60 percent. Spin for 15 minutes at 65 to 75 percent of max, then repeat the interval sequence. Do this series (2/2/15) three times. Use the last 15-minute spin as your cool-down.

FRIDAY
TIME: 60 minutes or less
GOAL: Rest or recover

Follow Monday's plan.

SATURDAY
TIME: 60 to 120 minutes
GOAL: Race or hard group ride

If you don't race, do a ride that requires varied intensity but keeps you around 85 percent of max most of the time. You want to simulate a race pace.

SUNDAY
TIME: 60 to 120 minutes
GOAL: Recovery ride

After yesterday's thrashing, your body will recover better with a light workout rather than total rest. Ride easy terrain at 55 to 65 percent of max, going easier and shorter if you feel totally worked—don't give in to the temptation to do nothing.

THE SERIOUS RACER READY TO KICK SERIOUS BUTT

You race at least once a month in season (or plan to after some success with a less-rigorous schedule last year). Through racing experience in other sports, or from your experiments from last season's mountain biking, you understand the basics of training—long steady rides, hard short rides, and rest. You have the motivation to train daily, and the free time to devote up to 2 hours for most of your rides. You might have won a race, or snagged a podium spot a few times. Now you want to rage. **Total weekly training time for this program: 12 to 16 hours.**

MONDAY

TIME: 60 minutes or less

GOAL: Rest or recovery (from weekend)

Spin in easy gears on flat terrain (55 to 65 percent of max), go for a walk with your dog, or take the day off.

TUESDAY

TIME: 90 minutes

GOAL: Short intervals

Warm up for 30 minutes at 55 to 65 percent of max. Do a series of all-out efforts for 15 to 20 seconds, followed by 7 to 9 minutes of recovery. Do the series six or seven times, then cool down for 15 to 20 minutes.

WEDNESDAY

TIME: 3 to 4 hours

GOAL: Endurance

Ride varied terrain at easy to moderate intensity (65 to 75 percent of max).

THURSDAY

TIME: 3 hours

GOAL: Death by interval

Warm up for 30 minutes at 55 to 65 percent of max. Do a series of 2-minute intervals just below max (85 to 90 percent), followed by 2 minutes at 60 percent. Recover for 15 to 20 minutes, then repeat the interval sequence. Do this entire series (2/2/15) five times. Then launch into a 5-minute interval at 85 to 90 percent of max, followed by 3 minutes at 60 percent. Recover for 15 to 20 minutes, then repeat. Use the final 15-minute recovery as your cool down.

SHORT INTERVALS VS. LONG

The guiding rule for intervals: The harder the intensity the shorter the interval. Short, all-out intervals at race pace or higher train your body to produce more power and to function longer through the production of lactic acid (a by product of anaerobic work) by clearing it from your muscles faster than it normally would.

Really long intervals—10 to 30 minutes—increase your ability to ride aerobically. Aerobic training conditions your body to produce more power for a longer time before it goes into anaerobic function. Long intervals should be slightly below your race pace (10 to 15 beats per minute lower if you use a monitor).

FRIDAY

TIME: 60 minutes or less

GOAL: Rest or recovery

Spin in easy gears on flat terrain (55 to 65 percent of max), go for a walk with your dog, or take the day off.

SATURDAY

TIME: 60 to 120 minutes

GOAL: Race or hard group ride

If you don't race, do a ride that requires varied intensity but keeps you around 85 percent of max most of the time. You want to simulate a race pace.

SUNDAY

TIME: 90 minutes to 3 hours

GOAL: Recovery ride

After yesterday's thrashing, your body will recover better with a light workout rather than total rest. Ride easy terrain at 55 to 65 percent of max, going easier and shorter if you feel totally worked—don't give in to the temptation to do nothing.

RIDING FOR ADVENTURE

7

We begin mountain biking

to explore a new sport.

What we discover

is the world.

Ride a mountain bike long enough and you will watch black bears scamper up hillsides too steep for treeholds. You will lie flat on your back, pressing against the top of a mountain that rubs a black sky ripped with yellow slashes of electricity— electricity that raises the hairs on your neck and arms (something you always thought people made up) and that only through stupid luck does not kill you, but which you will always remember as one of the most beautiful moments of your life.

You will find silent forests minutes from crushing knots of people. You will literally climb into a cloud. You will ride on parched trails that minutes of rain turn to mud beneath you, a sliding mud more dangerous than anything you've ridden, and even that will be one of the great times of your life.

You will ride through foreign jungles thick with animals you hear but never see, dodging plants whose sap can kill you, and when you come back into whatever touristy town is closest you will have a different look to you than other visitors. They will know it as well as you do. There will be moments as hard as rock when you and your friends get lost or hurt on a strange trail, and those same moments will turn as sweet and soft as a nap in the grass after you persevere—when you are home telling the stories.

When you become a mountain biker, life moves at the speed of your wheels. You find an intimacy with the world you could never feel from inside a car, and a range of travel you could never achieve on foot.

Your mountain bike can take you to all these places—but only if you take it places. Travel with your mountain bike and the world belongs to you both.

The Small and the Classic

I try to take my bike (or at least my riding clothes) on any trip that lasts at least a couple days. I don't always succeed, and even when I do I usually end up unpacking clean shorts and jerseys from my bags when I get home. But sometimes everything works out and I pedal into small, strange, wonderfully satisfying adventures.

I've rolled across winter wheat fields in Indiana during snow flurries, snuck away from a conference in Seattle to ride a fresh race course the day before the official event, searched for singletrack along the Florida coast and instead found a beachfront rolling with dolphins in waist-high water.

Those unexpected and unique moments are true mountain bike adventures, and they're important to what being a mountain biker means. But there's another kind of travel experience too seldom tasted: riding the classic routes.

A classic route isn't just an area with great riding, though that's key. The classics mean something to mountain bikers. They help define the sport. They tell us what it is to be a mountain biker. You're not really one until you've ridden Moab, so goes one theory. Another exalts the birthplace of modern mountain biking— California's Marin County.

Some riders have long checklists of mandatory rides. I'm not going to ruin your life by suggesting such a thing. You can do that yourself—and you probably will if you ride long enough. I've simply compiled a reference to the undeniably classic—spots with great riding and equally alluring lore. Use it as guide to create your own list.

Although the rides at these classic sites are epic, the price of getting there—and being there—doesn't have to be. Once you buy your bike, you've swallowed the most significant expense in mountain biking. Unlike skiing or golf, you don't have to pay to play—even in the classics. You might spring for maps, a nifty water bottle, and a lizard tattoo that looks irresistible after a day of riding and a night of drinking, but the best part—the riding—is free. (At many ski resorts you can pay for summer lift access to the top, but that's different.)

Lodging can be anything from a tent to a ski-resort condo, but that's under your control (as is airfare). The point is, while riding the entire list of classics might be a dream, no single site has to be. Riding as many or as few as you want can be a reality. Not enough of us know that, and not enough of us ride classic trails.

Start planning your first trip now.

Crested Butte, Colorado

This ski town north of Gunnison isn't on the way to anywhere else. You're in Crested Butte because it's your destination. And if you're a mountain biker, you've made an excellent choice. Crested Butte was one of the birthplaces of mountain biking—in 1976 locals began riding fat-tire bikes over 12,700-foot Pearl Pass to Aspen. The annual Fat Tire Bike Week (mid-summer every year) is one of the sport's best festivals, and the Mountain Bike Hall of Fame is a must-see. The single-track is swoopy, fast, and technical—probably almost all too tough for true novices. But there are plenty of old mining roads for beginners with strong lungs to test. The trailheads begin no lower than 9,000 feet—so be fit or suffer. In September the aspens turn a blinding yellow; earlier than that, wildflowers rule. Your choice.

Nothing is easy in Crested Butte, but everything is beautiful.

JAMIE BLOOMQUIST, OUTSIDE IMAGES

Must-Rides: Trails 409 and 401, Pearl Pass, the Upper Loop, Snodgrass.

Maps, Bike Shops, and Information: Crested Butte Bike Trails Map (970/349-5120); Crested Butte Fat Tire Bike Week (970/349-6817); Crested Butte Mountain Biking Association (970/349-6817); Crested Butte Sports (970/349-7516); Gunnison National Forest and Bureau of Land Management (970/641-0471); Paradise Bikes and Skis (970/349-6324).

Durango, Colorado

Every ride begins in the shadow of the San Juan Mountains, usually somewhere around 6,500 feet, and each gets harder and prettier as you ascend. (That's true for many mountain biking Meccas.) Durango hosted the first world championships in 1990, but it's become legend by providing homes for some of the sport's greatest riders. Juli Furtado, John Tomac, Ned Overend, Bob Roll, Greg Randolph, Greg Herbold, Ruthie Matthes, Missy Giove, Daryl Price, Ranjeet Grewal, and Dave Cullinan are just the short list of pros who have tagged Durango's zip code onto their addresses. Imagine latching onto that group ride.

Must-Rides: Hermosa Creek, The World Championship Cross-Country Course (at the Purgatory Ski Resort), Colorado Trail, Kennebec Pass.

Maps, Bike Shops, and Information: Durango Area Mountain Bike Map (303/259-3874); Purgatory Ski Resort (303/247-

Durango is home to famous riders and too much singletrack to count.

JAMIE BLOOMQUIST, OUTSIDE IMAGES

9000); San Juan National Forest (303/247-4874); Trails 2000 (303/259-4682).

Mammoth Mountain, California

Aptly named for its place in mountain bike lore, this ski resort and the trails in the surrounding Sierra Nevada range draw more industry to its World Cup and national-championship races than any other. The product expo rivals the annual insiders-only trade show in scope, and companies always hype new stuff in the late summer/early fall event. There are more than 60 miles of trails on the mountain itself—and too many to count on the surrounding lands. But the trail most associated with Mammoth is the Kamikaze that plummets from an 11,053-foot peak. Pros clock 50 to 60 mph on the straights.

Must-Rides: Kamikaze (or the Ezaki-mak—the uphill version), Titus Canyon, Cottonwood Canyon, Echo Canyon.

Maps, Bike Shops, and Information: Mammoth Mountain Bike Park (619/934-0606); Mammoth Ranger Station (619/924-5500); Mammoth Sporting (619/934-3239); MAMBO (619/934-3708).

Marin County, California

The most famous mountain biking site in the world—the true birthplace of the sport—has more trails closed than open. Because of tremendous publicity (and population), the Bay Area has become a flash point for access issues. For more than a decade, hikers, equestrians, naturalists, and mountain bikers have argued over how to live together. Today, almost all singletrack in the area is closed to mountain bikes and a 15-mph speed limit (enforced by rangers using radar and road blocks) exists on most dirt roads—including those on Mt. Tamalpais. Even with all the bummers, Marin can still make your heart pound when your tires begin the descent down the legendary Repack, or the guy passing you on the climb is Joe Breeze, Charlie Cunningham, or another pioneer.

Must-Rides: Repack, B-52, Pine Mountain Loop, Hoo Koo E Koo.

Maps, Bike Shops, and Information: Bicycle Trails Council of Marin (415/456-7512); City Cycles (415/346-2242); Marin County Open Space District (415/499-6387); Mt. Tamalpais State Park (415/388-2070).

Moab, Utah

To the world, Moab is mountain biking. And the Slickrock Trail—a 12-mile loop on sandstone—is Moab. The slopes of solidified sand dune are steeper than any dirt trail—with traction so dialed it's eerie. The shelves, steps, ledges, Swiss-cheese sections, bowls, and arches are ultimate tests of your technical ability. All of that is true, but insiders know that better vistas, longer trails, and fewer riders can be found outside Moab in the Canyonlands district. Ride the classic of the classics because you must. But leave time for the stuff nobody at home has heard of.

Must-Rides: Slickrock Trail, Porcupine Rim, Amasa Back, Poison Spider Mesa.

Maps, Bike Shops, and Information: Grand County Travel Council (800/635-6622); Moab District Bureau of Land Management (801/259-6111); Moab Visitor's Center (801/259-8825); Rim Cyclery (801/259-5333).

THE NEW CLASSICS

Our list of classics is so select that we omitted approximately four gazillion trails more beautiful than anything you've ever ridden. There's always an emerging hot spot for sweet trails—in recent years Sedona (Arizona); Bend (Oregon); the Nantahala and Pisgah Forests (North Carolina); and Randolph (Vermont). For more information of where to find the latest and coolest rides that aren't quite classic yet, check out the trail guide section in the Resources appendix.

Moab is mountain biking.
The one, true Mecca.

Mount Snow, Vermont

This "mountain bike capital of the North-east" (it used to be the "mountain bike capital of the East" until West Virginia's Pocahontas County sliced off part of the pie) started the world's first mountain-biking school in 1988. Its rooty, wet, rocky, plunging cross-country race course has been hailed—and cursed—by pros as the most technically challenging in the World Cup and national series. Handling skill is important no matter where you ride, but Mount Snow demands a mix of slow-speed finesse and grace under power that few riders can combine. The annual Snow Tire Slalom in March—downhill racing on the slippery stuff—was another first in the sport. Probably the most notorious creation, however, is the Naked Criterium—a circuit race held at night during the annual pro-racing weekend. Wearing nothing but their bikes, riders compete in front of a five-deep wall of spectators. A few pros always jump in (most recently Missy Giove and Shaun Palmer). It's unofficial, it's illegal, it's probably a bad idea, but somehow it sums up much of mountain-biking culture.

Must-Rides: Professional cross-country and downhill race courses. More than 140 miles of singletrack are regularly upgraded and slightly rerouted—just be sure to take one that drops off the other side of the mountain down into the Somerset Reservoir.

Maps, Bike Shops, and Information: Brattleboro Velo Club (800/272-8245); Green Mountain National Forest (802/362-2307); Mount Snow Mountain Bike Center (802/464-3333); West Hill Shop (802/387-5718); White River Valley Trails Association (802/728-5747).

Pocahontas County, West Virginia

The southern part of the Monongahela National Forest is a thick and rolling Appalachian wood-land where you can climb for four miles without ever going so high that you start sucking thin air instead of the lush lowland oxygen most of us are used to. This combination of mountain-style riding and flatland-style breathing has made Pocahontas County a must. The trails might be more technical than those more widely lauded in Vermont, but what's special here is the atmosphere—an almost-heaven casualness amid moon-shine-sharp challenges. There's no pretension, no attitude, and mountain biking here is all about fun instead of styling. It's refreshing.

The annual West Virginia Fat Tire Festival, sponsored by the Elk River Touring

Mount Snow, like all of Vermont, is technical and tough, yet lush.

STEVE BEHR, OUTSIDE IMAGES

Center, is the homiest and most laid back in the country, and Prop's Run features what many consider the best technical downhill of them all—probably a stretch, but it's definitely one of one of the best east of the Rockies.

Must-Rides: Prop's Run, Bear Pen Loop, Tea Creek Mountain, Red Run Loop.

Maps, Bike Shops, and Information: Elk River Touring Center (304/572-3771); Gauley Ranger District (304/779-4334); Pocahontas County Tourism Commission (800/336-7009); Snowshoe Mountain Resort (304/572-1000); West Virginia Mountain Bicycling Assoc. (304/296-4925).

Getting Your Bike There

Cost isn't always the best way to decide how to get your bike to distant vacation

Skip Brown, Outside Images

West Virginia is still unspoiled. Hurry.

sites, but it usually is (for me, anyway). Here are your options when you can't drive.

* **Airline**. Advantage: Quickest and most direct method. Disadvantages: Must pack (and unpack and repack and unpack) your bike. Must find a place to stash your bike box while you ride. Transporting box to and from airport is a hassle—especially in a rental car. (An airline lost my bike returning from France—when I got it back three days later it wasn't in the box and had mangled derailleurs.) Typical cost: $50—each way—for domestic flights; free for international. (Some organizations, such as IMBA, have a deal with certain airlines to let members fly their bikes free.)

* **Shipping**. Advantage: Cheaper than flying, without the hassle of dragging the box around. Disadvantages: Slower than flying (my friends and I prefer three-day UPS, a compromise of cost vs. time). You must find a shop or hotel or friend to receive your bike. You must pack and unpack (etc.), and also stash the box for the return trip. Typical cost: $20 to $35 domestic; impractical and expensive for foreign trips.

* **Renting**. Advantage: Least hassle. Disadvantages: The rental bike might not be the perfect size or right for your style. Availability also can be trouble. Typical cost: $20 to $50 per day.

Bikes Fly Free—If You Lie

Airlines discriminate against mountain bikers by making us pay to transport our rigs. How can I say that? Because it's $50 each way if I fly my bike. But if I tell the airline my oversized baggage is an "exercise machine" (and if they don't check inside the box), my bike flies free. I've also claimed that my bike box was part of an exhibit for a trade show. Free flight. If you're caught, all you have to do is pay up. Make sure your box doesn't say anything about bikes on the outside and you'll have a good chance of slipping your sweet machine past the harried ticketing person. Another strategy is to check your bike at curbside, slipping the attendant five or ten bucks. That's worked for me, too.

Packing Your Bike

Hard-shell bike cases are divine forms of transport. Not much disassembly is required, your bike fits in the thing snugly, and the shell is bombproof. But the cases cost about $200.

Cardboard, however, is free, and almost as protective—if you know how to pack your bike.

* **Get a bike box.** Bike shops usually store the boxes new bikes are shipped in—that's what you want. If the shop wants to charge you for the box, find a different one—and give them all your business when you want something that costs money. Get the biggest box you can find, one that lets you keep the rear wheel mounted.

* **Prep your bike.** Remove the pedals and seatpost (keep the saddle attached). Remove the front wheel, take out the quick-release skewer and wrap it in plastic or newspaper along with your pedals. Remove the bar ends (or loosen them so you can move them around later when you're trying to fit the bike into the box). Remove the stem (with the handlebar attached). Stick a plastic brace into the fork dropouts to prevent bending (a bike shop should also have a brace you can use, though you might have to pay or promise to return it). Squeeze the front brakes together and secure them with a rubber band or tape.

* **Pad your bike.** With bubble wrap, strips of cardboard, or something else soft and pliable, cover the tubes in the main triangle of your bike, the chainstays, the stem/handlebar, and the fork. Put the chain on the large cog in back and the middle chainring in front (to retract the derailleurs yet keep some tension on the chain). Wrap a layer of tape or bubble stuff around the chain, and secure it down against the padded chainstay.

Pack and pad your bike so no metal rubs metal, nothing will shake loose, and pointy parts won't puncture the box.

* **Tie your bike together.** Loosen the cables and pull the housings out of the stops to create enough slack to let the stem/handlebar be slipped between the padded top and down tubes. (You want it to snug into your triangle and not stick out too much, or your bike will be too wide to fit in the box.) You'll probably have to play around with it to find the best fit. Once you're sure you can fit the thing in the box, zip-tie or tape the bar to the bike. (If you're not sure it'll fit, wait until you slide the bike into the box before securing the bar to the frame.) Tie one of the cranks (looping through the pedal hole) to a chainstay.

* **Cut cardboard reinforcements.** Slice up cardboard to make a piece the same size as your front wheel. When you put your bike in, you'll slide this between the wheel and the side of the box to prevent punctures. Also cut small, matchbook-size pieces to go between the rear quick-release ends and the side of the box.

* **Slide the bike in.** It fits? Cool. No fit? Rearrange it.

* **Slide the accessories in.** Slip the front wheel in. Wrap the saddle and seatpost in bubble wrap and drop the package beside the back wheel or inside the main triangle. Drop the package of pedals and the front quick-release into the box. Also: Write your name and telephone number on a piece of paper and *tape it to your bike*. If the box gets obliterated in shipment, you still want your bike.

* **Seal the box with packing tape.** Be sure to seal the bottom, too. Then look all around for cuts and scrapes and lay a strip of tape over those. Be especially free with tape on the corners. Write your name and address on three to five pieces of paper and tape them to the box.

The Non-Packing-List Packing List

Packing lists are stupid. You won't use the same stuff I do (although I believe everyone should travel with at least one boomerang and some surf tunes). Anyway, use these guidelines. I've found them useful on trips around the world and to the next town.

RIDING YOUR CONTACT POINTS

If you can't ride your own bike on your epic trip (or any trip) and you need to rent or borrow one, you should at least ride your own contact points—the places where you and your bike interact.

Most of the perception we have of our bikes comes from the three places we actually touch it—the saddle, the pedals, and the handlebar. If you can transfer these to a loaner, you'll feel like a homey—no fumbling with pedals, no freaky saddle to assault your buttocks, and no strange grips or unfamiliar shifters to discombobulate your hands.

Taking your saddle and pedals is easy, and most rental outfits will let you swap. The handlebar is messier—and usually impractical. Even simply swapping grips is a hassle. A better idea is to find a rental that uses the same shifting and braking systems you're used to.

The most important of the three is pedals. At the least, make sure the pedals on a rental are compatible with your cleats (or come with clips-and-straps if you're a purist).

* You need twice as many inner tubes and socks as you anticipate.
* Extra shoes, extra gloves. Because it always rains.
* Take half as many jerseys. They dry fast, and no one will remember what you wore two days ago.
* For trips with a mix of cold and warm weather, unbulk your bag by taking arm warmers instead of long-sleeve jerseys.
* Take a well-stocked mini-tool. If you don't have a good mini-tool, toss the necessary tools in a small bag and think about how smart you are: pedal wrench, Y wrench, chain tool, box wrenches appropriate for your bike, and a small adjustable wrench.
* Pump. Because the first time you assume, you're uninflated.
* Throw some extra cleat screws in a plastic bag and stash it in your bathroom kit or stuff sack. A trip-saver. No hype.

OUT THERE: WHY MOUNTAIN BIKING MATTERS

One day in Colorado you accidentally ride off the front of the group, everything clicking as you climb a long arc of singletrack that hangs like a scaffold on 10,000 feet of mountain face.

You roll over the top and follow the flow of the trail down to a distant green dot that becomes a meadow. You realize you should wait for your friends so you stop, pull your water bottle from its cage, brace your bike at a slant, and sit on the top tube, one arm resting on the handlebar, the other on the saddle.

You look back up the trail and think about how honed you felt, and you laugh. The sound echoes back at you, and that's when you finally look at the mountainside just a few feet in front of your face. The cathedral of rock you just descended stretches into the clouds. Beyond the clouds. Beyond anything you can understand or imagine.

You hadn't been aware of the background chirruping of insects and birds, but as you stare into the sky you notice its sudden absence. Your hand stops drumming the water bottle against the frame. Breath comes soundless into your lungs. In that silence, you swear the mountain takes a step toward you.

I know that can never happen. I know if it appears to happen it is really just a trick of the clouds in the breeze against an immense solidity. It can never happen, but I saw a mountain move. It happened to me.

Such things don't happen only to me, because mountain biking matters. Beyond fitness and adventure and self-esteem and whatever, mountain biking is about something. Everyone who loves riding discovers this.

Pro downhill racer Dave Cullinan knows. "There's this downhill jump at Lake Isabella, near my parents' house, that I absolutely love," he once said. "You get 40 feet of air. You launch off this drop-off, and you're airborne. One of the best things about it is that you don't know where you're going to land. It took me a long time to get my huevos together to actually do it. When you're in the air, your mind completely empties and you're just doing it. It defines everything I love about mountain biking."

If you get out there, you will find your moments. Mountains will envelop you, or diminish you to nothing, then raise you higher than the sky. As you search for those feelings you will become more fit than you've ever been, you will understand the earth and learn the names of plants and animals most people never notice, you'll discover which limits you created for yourself and which ones are real.

Mountain biking is not a spiritual quest. It's fun. It's play. Sport. But even without your intent—or consent—mountain biking will lead you back into yourself and then out into the world. It's not just the scale of the mountains that does this, or the intimacy between you and your bike. It's the scale of the mountains versus the intimacy of the bike.

When you are out there on a mountain bike, sometimes you think of nothing but riding—shift, cant the pedal, lift the front, slide forward—and that total immersion washes your mind free of the residue of daily life. Sometimes when you are out there, you think of nothing—and those are the times you ride best.

But sometimes you think about mountain biking itself. Those are the times you're closest to the thing we're out there chasing.

RESOURCES

Books—Maintenance and Repair

Bicycling Magazine's Complete Guide to Bicycle Maintenance and Repair by the editors of *Bicycling* magazine and *Mountain Bike* magazine. 1994. (Rodale Press: 610/967-5171)

Cuthbertson's All-in-One Bike Repair Manual by Tom Cuthbertson. 1996. (Ten Speed Press: 800/841-2665)

Cuthbertson's Little Mountain Bike Book by Tom Cuthbertson. 1991. (Ten Speed Press: 800/841-2665)

Books—Ride Guides and Trail Information

There are hundreds of regional trail books, many produced by independent publishers. We list here only national guides, series that include most regions, or guides to the guides (national-scope publications that list guidebooks by state or region).

500 Great Rail-Trails by Julie A. Winterich. Nationwide guide of multi-use paths created from abandoned railroads. Living Planet Press, 1993. (Available from the Rails-to-Trails Conservancy: 717/238-1717)

America by Mountain Bike. Series of 20 regional books covering all areas of the U.S. (Menasha Ridge Press: 800/247-9437)

Mountain Biking the Best 100 Trails. Series with emphasis on California and the West. (Fine Edge Productions: 760/387-2412)

Trailfinder 98. The best comprehensive guide in the world. (IMBA: 303/545-9011)

Books—Other

Bike Cult: The Ultimate Guide to Human-Powered Vehicles by David B. Perry. For bike fanatics. 1995. (Four Walls, Eight Windows: 212/206-8965)

Bobke: A Ride on the Wild Side of Cycling by Bob Roll. Freaky riding stories from the freak master himself. 1995. (VeloPress: 303/440-0601)

How I Learned to Ride the Bicycle: Reflections of an Influential 19th-Century Woman. Edited by Carol O'Hare. Amazing book written in 1893 by women's social reform movement leader Frances E. Willard. 1991. (Fair Oaks Publishing: 408/732-1078)

The Mountain Bike Way of Knowledge. Philosophy, humor, and skills from cartoonist William Nealy. 1989. (Menasha Ridge Press: 800/247-9437)

The Quotable Cyclist: Great Moments of Bicycling Wisdom, Insight & Humor. Edited by Bill Strickland. Cool things people say about bikes and riding. 1997. (Breakaway Books: 800/548-4348)

Festivals

Camp Winnawombat. Several weekends throughout the year, for women.
PO Box 757
Fairfax, CA 94978
415/459-0980

Chequamegon Fat Tire Festival.
September.
PO Box 267
Telemark Resort
Cable, WI 54821
715/798-3811

Crested Butte (Colorado) Fat Tire Week.
June–July.
970/349-6817

Julian Fat Tire Festival. May.
PO Box 2036
Julian, CA 92036
760/765-2200

Methow Valley Mountain Bike Festival.
October.
PO Box 147
Winthrop, WA 98862
509/996-3287

Mountain Bike Weekend Festival.
Held in Jim Thorpe, Pennsylvania, in June. For information send self-addressed, stamped envelope.
634 S. Spruce St.
Lititz, PA 17543

Pedro's New England Mountain Bike Festival. Held in Randolph, Vermont, in September/October. 802/728-5747

Team Big Bear Mountain Bike Races.
Write or call for schedule.
PO Box 2932
Big Bear Lake, CA 92315
909/866-4565

West Virginia Fat Tire Festival. August.
U.S. Highway 219
Slatyfork, WV 26291
304/572-3771

Winter Park Resort Mountain Bike Series. June/July/August.
Winter Park Resort, Competition Center
PO Box 36
Winter Park, CO 80482
970/726-1589

Instruction

Barnett Bicycle Institute. Maintenance and repair school.
2755 Ore Mill Dr., #14
Colorado Springs, CO 80904
719/632-4607

Elk River Touring Center. Riding clinics.
U.S. Highway 219
Slatyfork, WV 26291
304/572-3771

Mount Snow Mountain Bike School.
Riding clinics.
800/451-4211; 802/463-3333

United Bicycle Institute. Teaches maintenance and repair and framebuilding.
PO Box 128
Ashland, OR 97520
541/488-1121

Magazines

The Bicycle Trader. Advertises used and vintage bikes for sale or purchase.
510 Frederick St.
San Francisco, CA 94117
415/564-2304

Bicycling Magazine. Covers all aspects of cycling.
Rodale Press
33 E. Minor St.
Emmaus, PA 18098
610/967-5171

Bicyclist. Covers road bikes and road racing.
6420 Wilshire Blvd.
Los Angeles, CA 90048
213/782-2339

Bike Magazine. Covers mountain biking.
PO Box 1028
Dana Point, CA 92629
714/496-5922

Dirt Rag. Covers mountain biking with a
bias toward East Coast.
181 Saxonburg Rd.
Pittsburgh, PA 15238
412/767-9910

Mountain Bike. Largest and most
comprehensive mountain bike magazine.
Rodale Press
33 E. Minor St.
Emmaus, PA 18098
610/967-5171

Mountain Bike Action. Covers mountain
biking.
Fax 805/295-1278

VeloNews. Mountain bike, road and track
racing coverage.
1830 N. 55th St.
Boulder, CO 80301
303/440-0601

Mail Order Companies

Bike Nashbar. 800/627-4227

BikePro. 800/Bike-Pro

Colorado Cyclist. 800/688-8600

Performance. 800/727-2453

Third Hand/Loose Screws (bike parts).
541/488-4800

Treads Bicycle Outfitters. 800/5-Treads

Miscellaneous

**Mountain Bike Hall of Fame and
Museum**
PO Box 845
Crested Butte, CO 81224
970/349-6817

U.S. Bicycling Hall of Fame. Road bike
history.
166 W. Main St.
Somerville, NJ 08876
908/722-3620

Organizations

Adventure Cycling Association. Bike
maps, touring routes, travel information.
PO Box 8308
150 E. Pine St.
Missoula, MT 59807
406/721-1776

American Discovery Trail Society. Trail
info and advocacy.
PO Box 20155
Washington, D.C. 20041
703/753-0149

**International Mountain Bicycling
Association.** Mountain bike advocacy,
trail information, trail maintenance
program.
PO Box 7578
Boulder, CO 80306
303/545-9011

League of American Bicyclists. Bicycle
advocacy, with emphasis on road riding.
190 W. Ostend St., #120
Baltimore, MD 21230
202/822-1333

National Off-Road Bicycle Association.
Governing body for mountain bike racing.
USA Cycling, Inc.
1 Olympic Plaza
Colorado Springs, CO 80909
719/578-4581

Rails-to-Trails Conservancy. Bicycle
advocacy and trail building.
105 Locust St.
Harrisburg, PA 17101
717/238-1717

Women's Mountain Biking and Tea Society (WOMBATS). Encourages women to ride.
PO Box 757
Fairfax, CA 94978
415/459-0980

Woodswomen. Women's adventure travel association.
25 W. Diamond Lake Rd.
Minneapolis, MN 55419
800/279-0555

Touring Companies/Guides

Backcountry. Southwest, Rockies, West Coast.
PO Box 4029
Bozeman, MT 59772
406/586-3556

Backroads. World's largest, with rides all over the world.
801 Cedar St.
Berkeley, CA 94710
800/462-2848

Kaibab Mountain Bike Tours. Southern Utah and Colorado.
PO Box 339
Moab, UT 84532
801/259-7423

Rim Tours. First off-road touring company in Utah, and maybe in the world.
1233 South Highway 191
Moab, UT 84532
800/626-7335

Western Spirit. Great guides, with trails other people don't find in Utah, Colorado, and Idaho.
478 Mill Creek Drive
Moab, UT 84532
800/845-2453

INDEX

A
Adkins, Paul, 88
Adventure Cycling Association, 124
airing, 64–65
American Discovery Trail Society, 124
anticipation, 56–57, 95
B
backpacks, 21
balance, 48–50
Bend, Ore., 112
bicycle. *See* mountain bike.
Blue Marsh Lake, 37
books, 123
bottom bracket, 8
box, bicycle, 116
brake lever, 10
brakes, 8
    adjusting, 23
    choices of, 8
    front vs. rear, 31–32, 73–74
    not using, 72–74
    play in, 94
    using, 31–33
    while turning, 69
    braking:
    feathered, 62
    front vs. rear, 73–74
    maximum, 93–94
    modulated, 31–32, 34
Breeze, Joe, 4
Breezer, 4
brooks, negotiating, 78–79
bunnyhop, 65–66
butted tubes, 13

C
cable adjuster, 23
cadence, 84
Camp Winnawombat, Calif., 123
carbohydrates, 51
case, hard-shell bicycle, 116
chain:
    broken, 23
    lubrication of, 22
chainrings, 8, 86
chainstay, 8
    curved, 14
Chequamegon Fat Tire Festival, Wisc., 123
cleat screws, 118
climbing, 39–46, 57–61
    breathing for, 59
    long, 58–59
    restarting while, 43–44
    standing while, 40–42
    steep, 59–61
clothing:
    arm-warmers, 118
    jacket, 19
    jersey, 19, 118
    shorts, 18
    socks, 19, 118
    spare, 101
    tights, 19
    travel, 118
cockpit, length of, 12, 16
cogs, 8, 32
Cook, Don, 28, 73
components, levels of, 13, 14
compressions, negotiating, 76

cornering, 46–47
crank, 8, 29
crashing, 85–86
cross-country riding, 9
    suspensions for, 10–12
Crested Butte, Colo., 28, 73, 110–11
    Fat Tire Week, 123
Cullinan, Dave, 111, 121
curves, 42
D
"dancing," 50
derailleur:
    front, 8
    rear, 8, 24
descending, 44–46, 61–63
    weaving, 62
dismount, running, 94–96
downhilling, 12, 44–46
    braking for, 33, 45, 46
    suspensions for, 10–12
drinking, 52
drop-offs, negotiating, 76
Durango, Colo., 111–12
dynamic technique, 57
E
eating, 51–52
elbows, position of, 28, 29, 36
Elk River Touring Center, W.Va., 88, 123
emergency landings, 67
endurance, building, 102
environmental concerns.
        See trail responsibility.
equipment, 7–24
    performance and, 8

eyes, using, 30–31
eyewear, 11, 19
F
fat, 51
festivals, 124
Fisher, Gary, 4
fit, 14–16
floating, 74–80
flow, 88, 89
Foley, Dan, 50
food, 50–53
forks, 8, 9
    selecting, 13
frames:
    aluminum, 13, 14
    composites, 14
    steel, 13, 14
    thermoplastic, 14
    titanium, 14
fuel. *See* food.
Furtado, Juli, 111
G
Giove, Missy, 88, 111, 113
gloves, 18, 118
Gravenites, Steve, 22
Grewal, Ranjeet, 111
grips, 15, 16
    holding, 38–39
    traveling with, 118
guides:
    riding, 123
    touring, 126
gussets, 14
gyroscopics, 73–74
H
handlebar, 8
    gripping, 37–39
    width of, 16
hands, using, 27–28
heart rate, monitoring, 102
heart-rate monitors, 20
helmets, 16–17
Herbold, Greg, 111
history of mountain biking, 4–5
hop in place, 92
hubs, quick release, 8
hydration, 52
I
Iditabike Race, 31
instruction, 124
International Mountain Bicycling
    Association, 5, 53, 124
J
Julian Fat Tire Festival, Calif.,
    123
jumps, 65, 66, 67, 90–93
    dead, 92
    landing from, 67

K
kickout, 90
knees, position of, 28, 29, 36
L
landings, safe, 67
League of American Bicyclists, 124
lights, 20
line, 30, 57
    on curves, 42
lube, 17, 22
lubrication, 22–23
lunge, 63–64
M
magazines, 124–25
mail-order suppliers, 125
maintenance guides, 123
Mammoth Mountain, Calif., 112
Marin County, Calif., 112
Matthes, Ruthie, 111
messenger bag, 21
Methow Valley Mountain Bike
    Festival, Wisc., 123
Moab, Utah, 112
modulated braking, 31–32, 34
Monongahela National Forest, W.Va.,
    2, 74
Mount Snow, Vt., 113
Mt. Tamalpais, Calif., 4, 112
Mountain Bike Hall of Fame and
    Museum, 124
Mountain Bike Weekend Festival,
    Pa., 123
mountain bike:
    first, 4
    fit of, 14–16
    full-suspension, 9–10
    hard-tail, 9
    packing of, 116–18
    prices of, 13–14
    renting, 116
    rigid, 9
    sales of, 4
    shipping of, 116
mud, negotiating, 77–78
muscles, alternating, 59–60
N
Nantahala Forest, N.C., 112
National Off-Road Bicycle Associa-
    tion (NORBA), 100, 124
night riding, 3, 20
O
obstacles, rolling over, 34–37
Olsen, John, 29–30, 60
Olympics, 4
organizations, 125–26
Overend, Ned, 111
P
packing a bicycle, 116–18

Palmer, Shaun, 113
passing, 101
pedal ratchet, 85
pedals, 8, 21
    clipless, 21–22
    clips, 21
    strap, 21
    threading of, 20
    traveling with, 118
    types of, 12, 14
    wrench for, 19–20
Pedro's New England Mountain Bike
    Festival, Vt., 123
Pisgah Forest, N.C., 112
Pocahontas County, W.Va., 113,
    114–15
positions, 28, 29
Price, Daryl, 111
prices, bicycle, 12–14
protein, 51
publications, 123–25
pump (tire), 17, 118
R
races:
    kinds of, 99–100
    preparing for, 100–01
racing, 1–5, 9, 97–107
    bicycles for, 9
    license for, 100
    warming up for, 100
Rails-to-Trails Conservancy, 124
Randolph, Vt., 112, 124
Randolph, Greg, 111
recovery, 102
    vs. rest, 103
relaxed riding, 27–28, 34
renting a bicycling, 116
Repack, 4
repair guides, 123
rest, 102, 103
ride guides, 123
riding techniques:
    acceleration, 83
    anticipation, 56–57, 95
    balancing, 48–50
    "bungee," 60
    bunnyhop, 65–66
    cadence, 84
    climbing, 39–46, 57–61
    crashing, 85–86
    descending, 44–46, 61–63
    dismounting, 96–86
    dynamic, 57
    emergency landings, 67
    floating, 74–80
    guides to, 123
    gyroscopics, 73
    instinct and, 28

jumping, 65, 66, 67, 90–93
lunging, 63–64
passing, 101
pedal ratchet, 85
position, 28, 29
"ready" position, 28, 29, 35
relaxation, 27–28
rolling over obstacles, 34–37
rowing, 60–61
sidehill drop, 72
singletrack, 71–72
speed, 81–83
spinning, 42, 83–4
standing, 40–42
turning, 46–48, 66–70
See also under braking *and* terrain
   techniques.
right of way, 45, 53
Ritchey, Tom, 4
rock fields, negotiating, 74–75
Roll, Bob, 89, 111
rollers, negotiating, 43
roots, negotiating, 75–76
rowing, 60
Rules of the Trail, 53
ruts, 79–80

S
saddle, 8
   height of, 15
   position of, 16
   tilt of, 15–16
   traveling with, 118
   using, 29
   width of, 16
San Juan National Forest, Colo., 112
sand, negotiating, 77
schools, 124
Schwinn Excelsior, 4
seat. *See* saddle.
seat bag, 17
seat post, 8
seatstay, 8
Sedona, Ariz., 112
shifters, 8
   adjusting, 24
shifting, understanding, 32
shipping a bicycle, 116
shoes, 18, 118
Shogren, Gunnar, 74
shouldering, 96
shoulders, riding position of,
   28
sidehill drops, 72
singletrack techniques, 71–72
Slickrock Trail, Utah, 112
speed, 72–73, 81–83
   developing, 102

spinning, 42, 83–84
spokes, numbers of, 14
standing while climbing, 40–41
standover height, 15
stem, 8
   height of, 16
   length of, 16
steps, negotiating, 80
streams, negotiating, 78–79
style, riding, 88–89
suppliers, mail-order, 125
suspensions, 8–12, 13, 14
   full, 9–10
   front, 9
   high-pivot unified rear triangle
      (URT), 10, 11
   linkage, 11
   low-pivot unified rear triangle,
      10–11
   McPherson, 11
   sweet-spot unified rear triangle,
      10–11
   swingarm, 11–12
switchbacks, 69

T
Team Big Bear Mountain Bike Races,
   Calif., 123
techniques. *See* riding techniques
   and terrain techniques.
tenseness, overcoming, 27–28
terrain techniques:
   compressions, 76
   drop-offs, 76–77
   mud, 77–78
   rock fields, 74–75
   roots, 75–76
   ruts, 79–80
   sand, 77
   sidehill, 71–72
   steps, 80–81
   switchbacks, 69
   washboard, 80
   water crossings, 78–79
   See also under riding techniques
      and turns.
360 jumps, 90–91
tire, flat, 22
tire patch kit, 17
toe clips, 21
Tomac, John, 111
tools, 17, 118
   box wrenches, 20
   cable cutters, 20
   pedal wrench, 19–20
   workstand, 20–21
Tour de France, 5, 89
touring companies, 126

trackstands, 49
traction, 22
   climbing, 40
trail closures, 5; 53
trail responsibility, 53, 62, 70, 77, 78
training, 101–07
   rest from, 102, 103
   timing of, 102
tricks:
   dead jumps, 92
   hop in place, 92
   jumping, 90–91
   kickout, 90
   360, 90–91
tubes (frame):
   butted, 13, 14
   down, 8
   head, 8
   seat, 8
tubes (inner), 17, 101, 118
   repair kits, 17
   valve adaptors for, 18
turns, 46–48, 66–70
   high speed, 70
   off-camber, 68–69
   slow, 68–69
   switchback, 69
   tight, 69
24 Hours of Canaan Bike Race, 2

U
U.S. Bicycling Hall of Fame, 124
United Parcel Service (UPS), 116

V
valve adaptor, 18

W
washboard, negotiating, 80
water, drinking, 52
water bladder/hydration pack, 19,
   101
water bottles, 17, 52
water crossings, negotiating, 78–79
Wattle-Blower Trail, Australia, 61
West Virginia Fat Tire Festival, 98,
   114, 123
wheel drift, 70
wheelies, 34, 36–37
   speed, 92–93, 94
Wiens, Dave, 46
Winter Park Resort Mountain Bike
   Series, Colo., 123
Women's Mountain Biking and Tea
   Society (WOMBATS), 125
Woodswomen, 125
workstand, 20–21
World Cup, 4